With and

Also by Steven Payne and available from Xlibris:

Carrying the Torch
My Lost Prize
Love Letters: Great Literary Romances
Love Poems
Paperwork

With and Without

STEVEN PAYNE

Library of Congress Control Number: 2021914180

ISBN:	Hardcover	978-1-9845-9188-3
	Softcover	978-1-9845-9187-6
	eBook	978-1-9845-9186-9

Print information available on the last page.

Rev. date: 07/14/2021

To order additional copies of this book, contact:
Xlibris
UK TFN: 0800 0148620 (Toll Free inside the UK)
UK Local: 02036 956328 (+44 20 3695 6328 from outside the UK)
www.Xlibrispublishing.co.uk
Orders@Xlibrispublishing.co.uk
800286

In loving memory

Rhona Sonia Shafik

4 July 1951 - 17 November 2018

חיים שלי

זיכרונה לברכה

There is no purpose to a memoir, if it isn't honest.

—Joyce Carol Oates: *A Widow's Story*

Remembered happiness is agony;
so is remembered agony.

—Donald Hall, 'Midwinter Letter'

Every love story is a potential grief story. If not at first, then later. If not for one, then for the other. Sometimes, for both.

—Julian Barnes: *Levels of Life*

CONTENTS

Part One

The Presence – With

Chapter One

Once Upon a Time

> There is no lonelier man in death, except the suicide, than that man who has lived many years with a good wife and then outlived her. If two people love each other there can be no happy end to it.
>
> —Ernest Hemingway: *Death in the Afternoon*

Surely all the best stories begin with 'Once upon a time ...' Or so we might learn when we are very young.

Very well, then.

Once upon a time there was a young man who met a much older woman — thrown together by random chance, fortune, fate, the hand of God, Cupid's arrow, whatever may be your preferred explanation — and the two fell in love. They loved, quarrelled, made love, quarrelled again, were incredibly happy, were desperately sad, were furiously angry, were tenderly loving, at one point parted but soon came back together. In due course the woman, unfortunately, became ill and died, and the man who cared for her, equally unfortunately, had to survive a little longer without her. They lived together long and, despite the downs as well as the ups, largely happily, but not ever after. Nobody does. I was, and am, an exceedingly ordinary man who met someone utterly extraordinary and to whom something extraordinary happened.

*

In September 1997 I was a twenty-five year old still living at home with his parents in Earl Shilton, a large village — or a small town — a dozen or so miles south-west of Leicester. I had been (but at that time was not) employed, but I was living a settled and orderly existence in the house in which I had lived since the age of three. Since leaving college at the age of seventeen I had had several jobs but long-standing and at times very severe mental illness issues (primarily bouts of profound and incapacitating depression from my late teens, which is a whole other story entirely) saw me reliant on benefits to eke out a life of sorts.

In September 1997 my best friend Adam — we had met on a psychiatric ward two years earlier for much the same reasons — who was then working as a plumber took it into his head that he wanted to buy a personal computer to help him keep his accounts. We had a lengthy browse around Coventry's branch of PC World and then, later that same day, at a second near Leicester, inspecting sundry models. He didn't buy a PC that day; I did, laying out (if I recall correctly) over £700 on a Packard Bell desktop computer loaded with the then bang-up-to-date Windows 98. I had never before had the slightest interest in computing, not even in earlier years when so many of my contemporaries were absorbed in Commodore 64s and Sinclair Spectrums and the like, but when I had seen what they could do after being given a demonstration by a shop assistant I realised that this was something I had to have. *I need this in my life — I'm having one and having it today.* I'm not normally an impulse buyer (well ... not often, anyway) but that ostensibly rash decision, now seemingly so random and out-of-the-blue, was to be the catalyst that changed my life for ever — and infinitely for the better.

In late 1997 the World Wide Web wasn't exactly a novelty but it was still comparatively young and as I've said it was entirely unfamiliar territory to me. Use of personal computers amongst the general population wasn't a rarity as such — PCs have been around for a long time — but in comparison to today, when everybody and anybody has internet access on a piece of plastic small enough to fit into the pocket of their jeans, it was still relatively so and taking off big time. Getting a computer and going online was still something of A Big Deal. (I can't even recall the first time that I ever heard the terms 'internet' and 'World Wide Web' as I wouldn't have been interested when I did so). PC ownership was growing in popularity but was still comparatively uncommon, certainly by today's standards. Back in the days of dial-up I set about learning how to use this marvellous new toy and how to navigate what some people were still referring to as the information superhighway. Even in those days the Web was to me like the world's biggest library, where all the information there could possibly be was available literally at one's fingertips. It was like being introduced to crack; though an absolute beginner I was hooked immediately, an instant convert. I bought some books suitable for internet virgins (newbies as they were called back in my day, kids, or if you were really net-savvy, n00bs) but much of the learning process was simply trial and error, learning by doing.

Another thing that grabbed me from the off was chat rooms. Many of the originals are now defunct and rather a period piece, later on widely closed down amid fears over online sexual grooming of children and, to many, superseded by social media such as MySpace and later on the all-conquering behemoth, Facebook. But back in 1997 they were all the rage and Yahoo! Chat was my favourite — possibly one of the first websites I ever visited since the URL had been given in one of the aforementioned books; like a party without the face-to-face interaction and where you're free to join and leave whenever you like, close to perfect for an introvert like myself. In the bad old days of dial-up internet telephone charges were lower after 6:00pm; anybody of that generation who used a PC in those pre-broadband, pre-wi-fi days will remember (with some nostalgia perhaps though not necessarily with tremendous fondness) having to wait until six o'clock in the evening before logging on and hogging the phone line as after 6:00pm it was cheaper. Late Friday nights were always my favourite time; I would head out in the early evening to my local for a night's drinking and then, considerably well lubricated, lurch home, climb the stairs to my room, turn on the computer, log on and sign in to Yahoo! Chat where my drunken alter ego would be the life and soul of the online party into the early hours of Saturday.

It was in this manner that within weeks of buying the PC I met a couple, ten or a dozen years older than myself, called Caron and Nigel Eagling who lived in a, to me, previously barely-heard-of town in Hertfordshire called Stevenage. At the time I'm not sure I was properly aware even of where Hertfordshire was let alone what Stevenage was like. Still, over the days and weeks Carol and Nigel became online friends and it was through them that they 'introduced' me to a close Stevenage friend of theirs called Rhona. You've got to meet Shaker (my online screen name back in the day, taken from the song 'Shakermaker' by the then hugely popular band Oasis) in Yahoo! Chat, they said; he's hilarious, they said; he's an absolute scream, they said; you should talk to him, especially on a Friday night when he's just in from the pub, they said. Late on Friday December 12th 1997 Rhona and I 'met' — virtually, of course — in Yahoo! Chat for the first time.

I'm trying to cast my mind back nearly twenty-two years to those heady days of drunken Friday nights in Yahoo! Chat and how Rhona (who never cared for the frivolous small talk of chat rooms, though we would never have met without her participation in it) and I began talking, but I can't remember the specifics as most of the time, at least to begin with, I was fairly uniformly pissed. Nevertheless things moved fast — very fast indeed. Presumably via email we soon swapped photographs; my twenty-five year-old self sitting in a chair in a corner of my room to Rhona (a photograph that Rhona kept in her purse and which I still have); in return a smiling Rhona in a floral print dress (at what I later found out was a bar mitzvah) flanked by her mother and auntie Sheila. Rhona was curvaceous, dark- and curly-haired, bespectacled, highly attractive in my eyes (not so much in her own; in one exchange she called herself 'mumsy') … and close to twenty-one years older than myself — in all honesty, old enough to have been my mother given that Rhona was almost twenty-one years old when I was born. I think I must have known about the disparity in age from the word go but since at this very earliest of stages our interaction was entirely virtual I paid it no mind at all. It never bothered me later on either, come to that.

There was no indication as yet that this was going to go anywhere further than drunken fun times online. I would very quickly discover that, twenty-one months a widow after a twenty-year marriage, still relatively young and attractive (certainly to me), Rhona had gone online almost on the same day that I did. She had recently begun to venture back onto the dating scene; indeed, by her own free admission she was playing the field and I was only one amongst several men that she had met up with, some more seriously and enduringly than others. My most serious rival was a successful Hounslow-based solicitor, handsome, charismatic and wealthy. I wasn't looking for or even thinking in terms of any kind of actual relationship. It just wasn't on the radar. And in any case, even if it had been, clearly I, a twenty-five year-old, broke, unemployed man with mental health issues and of (at best) decidedly average looks from the arse end of nowhere stood absolutely no chance.

I was wrong.

Chapter Two

A Night on the Island

> There is nothing more admirable than when two people who see eye to eye keep house as a man and wife, confounding their enemies and delighting their friends.
>
> —Homer: *The Odyssey*

Much like computer use, in 1997 the now-ubiquitous mobile phone was nowhere near as common as it would become (and they were notoriously large and cumbersome, by today's standards comically so). It would be another couple of months before I owned my first ever brick-like mobile phone but alongside the purchase of the PC I made further concession to the digital age by getting hold of a BT Lyric pager, a nifty little device which received text messages (but did nothing else; it was, in effect, like a mobile phone which had no phone function and could only receive texts). The person trying to send you a message called a certain number and spoke to an operator (yes, a real live person) who took the message and had it converted by the magic of telecommunications wizardry to a text message delivered — when it worked, which in certain areas could be decidedly hit and miss — to said device. Quaint, even primitive by today's standards, of course, but in its day I thought that this was rather neat. To this day I make few phone calls but am a dedicated text maniac; I've still never quite got over the witchcraft of sending written messages through the air from one piece of plastic to another, potentially on the other side of the planet. I may not be the world's biggest technophile but I'm clearly easily amused.

Precisely one week after first speaking to each other online Rhona and I met in person for what was — to put it bluntly, but there's no purpose to a memoir if it isn't honest — a one night stand. In years to come Rhona wondered, fairly often and aloud, what kind of madness possessed her to take a chance on leaving the kids to be looked after by Caron and Nigel and to drive eighty miles up the motorway to a Midlands town she had never heard of for what was effectively a quick bunk-up — and might never have been anything more than that — with a total stranger nearly twenty-one years her junior she had 'met' online exactly one week previously. Rhona was a widow but not dead from the waist down and that surely played a large part in it. All the same she and I agreed to meet face-to-face for the first time in Hinckley (a large town a few miles from Earl Shilton) in the evening of Friday December 19th 1997, exactly a week almost to the hour after we had been introduced online. I never have learned to drive — at seventeen I had had a few informal lessons from a family friend but I never applied for the test — so I got a minicab. In Hinckley market place there was a pub named The Bounty, still in existence, in which I used to drink occasionally at that time and it was while in there, in the noise and heat and crush (and in those far-off days, smoke) of a full boozer on a Friday night, that my pager received a message to say that Rhona was waiting for me in her car outside Hinckley's long since defunct branch of McDonalds a few hundred yards away. As I recall it was something like: *metallic blue Proton*, the message read in part. *Registration number H167 DCU.*

I've made a point of recording these two dates in December because they're the closest thing to an anniversary that Rhona and I had — not one anniversary but two anniversaries. Since we lived a relatively unconventional life and had a relatively unconventional relationship — we never formally married, which personally I would have done and will always regret that we did not — we had to fall back on the two dates which came closest to a wedding anniversary; December 12th when we were introduced online and December 19th when we met in person and spent a torrid night together. Unlike couples who have a legal marriage we didn't generally do anything in particular to celebrate these two dates — we didn't go out for dinner or exchange cards or anything of that nature — but they were always noted by me. And always will be.

I digress. I left The Bounty and walked across the market place to where the car described in the pager message was parked outside McDonalds. I climbed into the passenger seat; in the driver's seat sat Rhona, far more attractive in the flesh than her photographs had made her look, wearing a black shirt (referred to by Caron Eagling as her 'shagging blouse') and I don't recall what else, whether it was trousers or a skirt.

Sex was clearly on the agenda but we needed somewhere to go; I cast around for ideas and came up with what was then called the Island Hotel (it has changed hands and names several times in subsequent years), a large and rather exclusive hotel on the A5 on the outskirts of Hinckley, very close to the junction with the M69. We had no reservation but on arrival we managed to get a room for the night and so we spent our first face-to-face encounter in an anonymous albeit relatively luxurious hotel room. A lot more than face to face, come to that, but over certain things I shall draw a veil of modesty.

As for her first impressions of me on that Friday evening, in later years Rhona would often say that she initially thought I was "funny-looking" — her usual description of me; not so much ugly as "funny-looking" — but was attracted by the fact that pinned to the sweater beneath my black biker's jacket I was wearing a red AIDS ribbon, common at that time. Rhona — who had the strongest social conscience of anyone I've ever known — took this as a sign of tolerance, care and compassion. (She was right. Why else would anyone wear an AIDS ribbon?). It was the kind of thing that Rhona herself would do; it was a sign that we were vibrating on the same wavelength and in so many matters and on so many issues thought alike. It was the laying of foundations, after a fashion.

Because I acquitted myself honourably in bed with none of the issues that can beset the nervous newbie I don't believe that Rhona ever knew, never suspected — not even to her dying day — that she was the first woman I had ever made love to; that on that Friday night, December 19th 1997, she had taken my virginity. Nobody else knows this either and I say it here for the first time. Although unconscionably late in the day I had reached the age of twenty-five still virgin; with some past sexual experience certainly but as I say, Rhona was the first woman I had slept with. She never knew and I never raised the issue — I was ashamed of still being a virgin at twenty-five given that the average age of losing one's virginity is around seventeen or eighteen — but nevertheless, it is a fact. Should I have told her? I still don't know. As far as I'm aware she never knew; certainly I never raised it.

In the morning I settled the bill; oddly I can't remember if we had breakfast or not. Rhona took me back to Earl Shilton — parking a few yards away from the house — before carrying on back to Stevenage.

Our night on (always *on*; definitely *on*, not *at*) the Island, as Rhona would always later refer to it, could have been no more than a single, highly enjoyable but brief episode. I could have gone about the rest of my life and Rhona could have gone back to the dating scene and neither of us might have seen each other ever again. That 'night on the Island' would become part of our own personal lover's story; after our move to Leicestershire in 2000 every time that we drove past it, as we did relatively often, we would hold hands in remembrance of our first night together. And yet, and yet … I don't know what on earth it could have been but there must have been something or other about me since, even though we had confessedly had a one night stand which could have been the beginning, middle and end of it all, Rhona and I kept in touch over Christmas 1997. There was *something*, some indefinable connection between us to which we typically apply the term, for want of a better, 'chemistry', something that kept us wanting to stay in touch; a meeting of minds, a vibration on the same wavelength. Rhona always claimed that a major part of this was my intelligence since from my schooldays I'd had a reputation for being 'a bit clever'. I had had only a decidedly average state comprehensive education and was academically undistinguished. I hated school with a passion and regarded it as a waste of my time; I could have been at home reading and actually learning interesting things. Anything I had picked up came not from school but from a native curiosity about the world which I nourished by reading voraciously, reading almost anything that I could lay my hands on touching on all the things that interested me, from a very early age. Rhona would fairly regularly embarrass me deeply by saying to others, in my presence: "I'll never know as much at my age as Steven does at (insert my age here)". She was doing herself a disservice; Rhona herself was acutely, supremely intelligent, highly mentally or intellectually alert, always hungry to know and to understand — we would never have become involved otherwise. We regarded a day without learning something new, even if only a word with which we'd been previously unfamiliar, as a day wasted. I'm duty bound to say that Rhona, while the warmest, kindest and gentlest of people, was incredibly bright and had limited patience with the less intellectually able. She didn't tolerate fools gladly or easily, in short. I admit that it's not the most attractive or appealing trait in the world but I'm the same.

So there was definitely a spark or rather much, much more than a spark from the word go. Moreover at some point around Christmas 1997 Rhona invited me down to this unknown place called Stevenage for a small party she was throwing on New Year's Eve. Although no party animal I definitely wanted to see Rhona again — a mutual desire, clearly — and I was more than glad to see out 1997 and see in 1998 with her and a modest gathering of her friends, Caron and Nigel included. (Rhona's kids were packed off for the night with another Stevenage friend; Rhona had plans for the later part of our night that definitely didn't involve two teenagers hanging around). I packed a bag with a few essential things for a day or two and on the last day of 1997 took the train from Leicester down to Stevenage via Peterborough.

I had a couple of changes of underwear in a bag, a change of clothes and some toiletries. I expected to be going to a party, would probably get a bit drunk, be hungover the following day, stay perhaps a day or two at the most then make my way home. I hadn't the faintest idea that I was going to what would overnight become my new home for the next three years and the start of the relationship of a lifetime with the love of my life and soulmate.

Chapter Three

Getting to Know You

> You put together two people who have not been put together before; and sometimes the world is changed, sometimes not. They may crash and burn, or burn and crash. But sometimes, something new is made, and then the world is changed. Together, in that first exaltation, that first roaring sense of uplift, they are greater than their two separate selves. Together, they see further, and they see more clearly.
>
> —Julian Barnes: *Levels of Life*

The party was a great success. Rhona's home in Archer Road in the Pin Green area of Stevenage was spacious and tasteful, the food and drink flowed and the company enjoyable. For all that, Rhona was glad to see the last partygoer depart late that evening (or rather early the next morning, the first day of 1998) because as soon as the door was closed she pounced on me and we hurried upstairs to the bedroom. There would be a great deal of pouncing in those early days, as Rhona would later recall with a smile. We didn't surface until well into lunchtime the following day — the first day of 1998 — as the house was beginning to fill again with the guests who had been invited over for a New Year's

Day breakfast which due to our tardiness was eventually served up, my diary records, at 3:30pm.

I'd gone down to Stevenage with enough clean clothing and toiletries for a few days since that's how long (at the very most) I expected to stay, but the days accumulated and Rhona showed no sign of wanting me to leave. If anything very much the opposite. In fact I stayed so long that eventually we had to venture into Stevenage town centre for me to buy an emergency supply of new clothing to tide me over until such time as I caught the train and went back to Earl Shilton.

Which I did briefly and occasionally, but it eventually became clear that I had for all practical intents and purposes unwittingly left home on New Year's Eve 1997 and made Archer Road, Stevenage, my new home and had started a new life with Rhona. I simply had no idea whatever and could never have foreseen that when I climbed aboard the train at Leicester station on the last day of 1997 I was leaving home and journeying into a new life, but that's precisely how it panned out. In essence I went down to Stevenage for a New Year's Eve party and never went home — or rather Stevenage in general and Archer Road in particular become my home. Trips to Leicestershire were in the nature of short visits back to see the family; Rhona and I never (at least as far as I can recall) formally declared to each other that we were now in a serious, exclusive and committed relationship — my first and I expect and intend it to stay that way — and were living together: we simply fell into it piecemeal, day by day, Rhona giving up on her previously wide-ranging dating, even on the rich and handsome Hounslow solicitor. It was unspoken but somehow we had become an item, a pair, a couple. I had, in her words, somehow "crept in under the wire." This was as much of a surprise to me as it was to Rhona, if not more so. I don't know which one of us was more amazed; after all when we met it wasn't as though I had been looking for love. I'd had absolutely no plans of embarking upon a relationship. I wasn't actively looking for anyone to settle down with; it simply happened. I had met someone who had been a totally random stranger — more than two decades older than myself, widowed and with two teenaged children, eighty-odd miles away — and out of nowhere had found myself falling in love. Rhona occasionally used to say that if someone had written the story of how we met as a work of fiction nobody would take the plot at all seriously since everything about it was not merely so random but just so unlikely, improbable, implausible. And yet there we were. It was no fiction; it happened.

Like the soppiest of couples we had our pet names for each other: to Rhona I was 'Weeven' or 'Weev' whereas Rhona had already been given her nickname ('Wowo' or simply 'Wo') many years before by a school friend, though in addition I called her 'dumpling' and 'sweet tart' — my cheeky version of *sweetheart*. Now that we were an item we were no longer Rhona and Steven but RhonaandSteven or Weev and Wo; Team Wowo as she sometimes put it.

Rhona and I got to know each other, our pasts and our current lives the way that couples generally do: gradually.

Rhona Sonia Goldstone was born in Ashton-under-Lyne (since 1974 part of Greater Manchester but historically in Lancashire) on July 4th 1951 but raised in a liberal, secular Jewish home in Geordieland — specifically the seaside town of Whitley Bay on the north-eastern coast, latterly with her slightly younger brother Clive. Rhona's father, Leslie, had come from exceedingly humble beginnings in Bolton; her mother, Zena, had been a child refugee from Holland in the 1930s as astute Jews saw which way the wind was blowing with regard to the rise of the Nazis across Europe. In complete contrast to the poverty in which Leslie had been raised Zena felt that she came of more genteel stock. It was a standing joke in the family, and something about which I often teased Rhona, that she too had been raised in affluent upper-middle-class-dom; as a child (at what I ribbed her was called Goldstone Towers — actually a semi-detached house in Davison Avenue, close to the sea front) her parents employed a maid, for example.

There were relatively few senses in which Rhona thought of herself as a Geordie; she had a neutral, unplaceable, generic north-of-The-Wash-to-Severn accent, flat vowels and all, but never acquired the distinctive north-eastern dialect (though inevitably, growing up surrounded by it, she could put it on at will). Nevertheless for her Whitley Bay had been home, the place where she spent her formative years amongst the sticks of rock, candyfloss, fish and chip shops, the Venetian café and the

Spanish City and its annual summer influx of tourists, especially from Scotland, when the sea fret and frigid winds were not (or were) blasting in from the North Sea. Although she didn't (in my hearing) call herself a Geordie, the north-east of England would always tug at her; she was a dedicated fan of the various series' of *Auf Wiedersehen, Pet*, for example. As she would reminisce decades later, schooldays at Valley Gardens could be difficult as she was sometimes bullied for being overweight — her weight being a great issue for her when young; in Birmingham in 1974 Rhona would undergo major surgery, an intestinal bypass carried out with the aim of losing weight — but she made a bold move to the capital at eighteen when London was still swinging as the Sixties drew to a close; her detailed diaries of that time list amongst many other things the music that she was listening to (exactly the same guitar-based bands such as Cream as I had and did — another factor that drew us together). She was active in and a supporter of the then relatively nascent gay liberation scene (homosexuality had been decriminalised in England and Wales just a few years before), moving at one point into a gay commune and later a house in Kilburn's Brondesbury Road.

Rhona had been born at a black-and-white time when confectionery, sugar and meat were all still rationed but she came of age and was very much a child of the 1960s, never quite losing the free-wheeling, socially liberal hippy ethos even when later outwardly appearing to live the most conventional of married, childbearing, suburban, semi-detached lives. Rhona was born at exactly the right point in the baby boomer generation; she turned 16 just as the summer of love was flowering and reached the age of majority in 1969, the year of the Woodstock festival, a few weeks before Armstrong and Aldrin walked on the moon. The following year she was one of the estimated 600,000, possibly 700,000 at the legendary 1970 Isle of Wight Festival at the end of August featuring amongst many others Kris Kristofferson, Supertramp, Taste, Procul Harum, Joni Mitchell, Miles Davis, Emerson, Lake and Palmer, The Doors, The Who, Free, Donovan, Pentangle, The Moody Blues, Jethro Tull, Joan Baez, Leonard Cohen and one of the last performances of Jimi Hendrix who would join the 27 Club just a few weeks later. Like many of her contemporaries Rhona wasn't unused to ingesting illegal substances and she said that she slept through much of it. That aside, defying the old dictum, Rhona remembered the Sixties and was there. Years later, after gaining her B.Ed from the University of Middlesex a succession of jobs followed, none of them especially long-lasting; the civil service; bar work in a pub to make ends meet; even a brief spell as a teacher.

Rhona had had boyfriends but in 1976 she met, then working in a café in London, a young Egyptian (a Coptic Christian rather than Muslim), four years her junior, voluminous afro, sprayed-on cheesecloth shirt and flares and all, born as Emad Shafik in El-Mahallah El-Kubra, the largest city in the Nile delta, but anglicised as John and thereafter always known as such. He was smitten from the very start whereas Rhona was more cautious, yet his persistence paid off; the two met over an unsolicited coffee that he bought for her, fell in love, and in November of that year were married. Rhona always told me that she felt somewhat bounced into a wedding she had never particularly wanted; still largely the free-spirited, free-wheeling hippy of the previous decade marriage was viewed as decidedly square, but when John got a licence and showed up one day in his best suit she went along with it. (The irony of a Jewish girl marrying an Arab, albeit a Christian Arab, was never lost on her). Children followed; a daughter, Leah, was born in London in 1981 and a son, David, born in Hitchin in Hertfordshire in 1984. In time John rose above his earlier lowly occupations and became a highly qualified telecommunications engineer; the family moved to a leafy area of the new town of Stevenage in Hertfordshire within relatively easy reach of London without the capital's expense, traffic and pollution.

For years life rolled along placidly and contentedly; greatly to her surprise Rhona the hippy found herself living the quiet life of a suburban housewife and Earth mother, cooking and cleaning — keeping house as they say — and all the rest of it. Eventually however life threw the happy family a curveball, as it is wont to do and as I would find out in the worst possible way many years later. At the age of just thirty-five John developed a rare condition graced by the tongue-twisting name of hypothalamic neurosarcoidosis. This unusual disease involves the formation of lesions in various parts of the body; in this case, specifically, the hypothalamus and pituitary glands of the brain. Over the course of the next several years it caused personality changes — as Rhona was the first to say bluntly, on occasion John was frankly away with the fairies —, odd and obsessive behaviour, the onset of diabetes, narcolepsy and very significant weight gain in a formerly slim man. As Rhona put it, John, at intermittent intervals, lost his mind and spent some lengthy periods in London hospitals.

John was ill for five years. On the morning of Wednesday March 13th 1996 — the same day as the horrific gun massacre in Dunblane — Rhona and John went to the dentist, always a source of dread and terror to Rhona who was very severely dental-phobic all her life (to the extent that she refused to watch any dental scenes on TV and would immediately turn the set over or off). Back at home John went upstairs while Rhona watched the terrible news from the Scottish primary school unfold on TV. After a while Rhona became aware that John had been absent for an unusually long time; she ventured upstairs to find him dead in the bathroom. He was forty years old. In the blink of an eye Rhona was a widow at forty-four and her children without a father.

Chapter Four

Life

> Life is what happens to you while you're busy making other plans.
>
> —widely attributed to John Lennon, but actually Allen Saunders

When we met I was an old twenty-five and Rhona a youthful forty-six. At time of writing I'm the age that Rhona was when we met and I feel as old as the hills. Rhona did not. There's an unwritten 'rule' about age-gap relationships to the effect that you shouldn't be with anyone who is half your own age plus seven years. If Rhona and I had taken any notice of this 'rule' we wouldn't have become involved since I would have had to have been thirty, whereas, as already mentioned, I was in fact twenty-five. Personally the age gap of almost twenty-one years was never an issue as far as I was concerned; I never saw or thought about any discrepancy of this kind. I fell in love with a person, not an age. I thought, felt and believed that we were an evenly-matched couple who in terms of age more or less met up somewhere in the middle. When I looked at Rhona I simply saw Rhona rather than someone more than two decades older than myself; if a May-to-December relationship had ever been a problem for me (or indeed for Rhona) we would never have become involved in the first place. Still, there were some times when the age gap intruded itself upon Rhona rather than on me; on a number of occasions (at least until I grew a beard) while out shopping I was mistaken by salespeople for Rhona's son, which I found fairly amusing but which Rhona found distinctly uncomfortable. It didn't bother me in the slightest but Rhona was discomfited, at least to begin with until the years began to catch up with me, the hair retreated and my beard began showing distinct traces of grey.

Life in Stevenage was, to mix my metaphors, a learning curve and something of a culture shock. I had grown up — had spent my first quarter of a century in fact — on the edge of what was then straddling the indistinct line between a large village or very small town where vistas of wide open countryside were a few minutes' stroll away; now I found myself living eighty miles south in the heartlands of home counties suburbia where the people talked funny and said *barf* instead of *bath* and *grarse* instead of *grass*. Now life was not horses, cows and sheep in a patchwork of fields more or less at the end of my street but traffic, noise, pollution, people, the hurly burly of a large southern town. I didn't mind as I was with Rhona, which is all that mattered; it was simply different. I was in no danger of becoming a townie (as though one can become one; one either is or is not) but I enjoyed my three years in Stevenage and I retain a deep and abiding affection for the place because of its associations for me. Like other new towns (and plenty of old ones) it doesn't exactly have much in the way of glamour or excitement and, also like other new towns, has a reputation for being something of a soulless concrete jungle; but its charm for me is that it is where Rhona and I began and where we would share our lives for the best part of three years. There was more to Hertfordshire than Stevenage in any case; it's an extremely lovely county in parts and in the more clement months of the year we enjoyed going out and about, touring the rural corners as the fancy took us.

Stevenage is carved up unequally into the small Old Town — traditional and picturesque in parts — and the much larger New Town. As post-war regeneration in Attlee's Labour government got underway the Patrick Abercrombie Plan (technically the *Greater London Plan* of 1944) had called for a ring of new towns surrounding London to get 380,000 people, very often living in abysmal conditions, out of the war-ravaged capital; under Lewis Silkin, Minister of Town and Country Planning, Stevenage, thirty miles north of London, became the first place in the UK to be thus designated in November 1946 under the New Towns Act. There was widespread and vociferous opposition from local landowners and others; at an incredibly hostile public meeting Silkin told a testy 3,000-strong crowd: "It's no good you jeering. It's going to be done" and had to be taken from the building by a police escort. Initially the opponents' case was upheld but was subsequently rejected on appeal and the New Town was sanctioned by the House of Lords in July 1947. The idea was that new Stevenage would house around 60,000 people in neighbourhoods of ten thousand each, intended to create a distinct sense of community. (Unsurprisingly the current population is creeping towards 90,000 as the town expands inexorably to the north and west). The first houses started to be built in September 1949 to an unusual design by the planner Gordon Stephenson and the architect Peter Shepheard intended to keep cars — this was an era of burgeoning car ownership — and pedestrians apart as far as possible, with numerous footpaths and cycle lanes; many houses in the town were planned in such a way that they do not face directly onto a road, for example. Stevenage also had Britain's first purpose-built pedestrianised town centre. (For his pains Silkin was raised to the peerage as Baron Silkin of Dulwich in the 1950 Birthday Honours list).

Rhona and I had been together for barely a couple of months when at the end of February 1998 we decided — some might say rashly — to go abroad on holiday, eventually alighting on Tunisia. Rhona had been very well-travelled since childhood, criss-crossing Europe with her parents and brother on family holidays and much later, when married to an Egyptian, making several visits to Egypt (picking up some reasonable conversational Arabic in the process), but this was my first ever trip overseas and my first flight. (To date it remains the only one. I'm not much of a traveller and now think of my holidaying days as over). Landing at Monastir airport we had an extremely enjoyable week staying at the rather splendid Tej Marhaba hotel in Sousse, somewhat marred by the fact that on the final morning of the holiday Rhona wanted to visit an open-air market and even though it was the end of February I got a nasty case of sunstroke which I'd never experienced before and made me feel extremely ill for days after we got home; as the day wore on and the time for our departure from Monastir airport approached I felt increasingly poorly and I was semi-conscious and groaning on the return flight to Stansted. That aside the experience was a positive one, although as a vegetarian in a country where (as with so much of the Arab world) few people understand the rationale for willingly and deliberately refraining from eating meat and fish I more or less lived on continental breakfasts and omelettes for all meals for the week. (It took me some considerable time to be able to face an omelette again). The Arab world was alien but fascinating and Sousse an interesting old town with a fantastic *souk*. Rhona would go abroad again many more times in her life though not with me; I was always content to live the experience vicariously through her long and detailed emails, texts and photographs home. Until our four-month separation over the winter of 2014-15 we never spent longer than about two weeks apart, typically on those occasions where Rhona went over to the States to visit David and his wife.

Rhona and I shared not only our lives but many interests, although at times she found it difficult to adopt or adapt to all of them. In the summer of 1998 we went away to the West Country on what was for me something of a musical and literary pilgrimage, taking in Down Ampney — the Gloucestershire village which was the birthplace of the composer Ralph Vaughan Williams —, the cathedral cities of Gloucester, Hereford and Worcester and several sites associated with Edward Elgar including several of his homes and also his grave. Rhona had no great liking for classical music but she gamely played along with my pet obsessions — even, on several occasions in our Stevenage years, travelling down into the capital to attend Proms concerts at the Royal Albert Hall on balmy summer evenings. It's possible that unless they've been wiped, somewhere out there in the ether there still exist a few BBC televised Proms concerts, dutifully recorded by us back in the distant days of VCRs, where (if you know where to look) we can be seen in the audience behind the presenter. This was a demonstration of love on Rhona's part as this wasn't her thing musically at all — she remains the only person I've ever known who could briefly fall asleep during a performance of Elgar's *The Dream of Gerontius* conducted by Andrew (later Sir Andrew) Davis and had to be gently nudged awake before she started to snore. Poor Rhona. This great work in particular seemed to have a permanently soporific effect; for years afterwards, lying next to each other in bed, she would ask me to hum the first few melancholy bars of this masterpiece of English music to put her to sleep. Though not her style of music she heard so much Vaughan Williams (along with Sibelius, my favourite composer) so often that she could identify the *Tallis Fantasia* or *The Lark Ascending* from the first few bars alone. Still, all successful relationships are about give and take and if Rhona gamely put up with my concert-going and cathedral-visiting I couldn't count the hours I lost over the years resignedly sitting in one clothes shop after another (Rhona, being a big lady of the more generous figure in those days, was especially devoted to Evans and Ann Harvey) while she tried on one item of clothing after another ... and another ... and another ... and another. Spouses everywhere will understand without further explanation. Rhona was to clothes what I was to books and CDs (that is to say, a fanatical and obsessive collector). Not only were her own wardrobes crammed full of clothing she (like many female spouses) enjoyed dressing me up too and she derived great pleasure in seeing me try on and buy threads of my own.

The following summer we spent a week tracking across the south coast, from Brighton in the east — a place with which both Rhona and I fell in love; its narrow lanes, its shops, its free and easy bohemian, rather louche atmosphere — to Newton Abbott (where one of Rhona's oldest friends lived) in Devon in the west. In both of these weeks in the summers of 1998 and 1999 we were almost unbelievably lucky; not merely blessed with glorious weather but — these adventures were largely unplanned and we played each day by ear — able to find somewhere, some boutique hotel or B & B, to lay our weary heads every night. They were, and are, some of the happiest times we ever knew.

The trip to Tunisia just a couple of months after Rhona and I met was, as I've said, my first and only venture abroad. Rhona would jet off to foreign climes a great many times in coming years albeit without me. I enjoyed exploring various corners of England and over our years together there would be a good many future breaks and trips. We sat by the murky, poisonous green waters in Bath; with the help of my favourite trusty walking stick Rhona hauled herself up the longer but less steep route to the top of a blustery and windswept Glastonbury Tor; we enjoyed a taste of the high life at a beautiful hotel near the sea in Sussex; we spent a few days at a luxury hotel not too far from home in Rutland; several days exploring Derbyshire; touring the Norfolk coast; visiting and revisiting Brighton, rambling around the narrow streets of York and so many, many more, all dutifully written up by me for the diary. Though not a religious man I can be as awestruck by the architectural genius of mediaeval buildings as anyone and inevitably I would want to visit attractive old churches and cathedrals to the extent that when away it became something of a standing joke between us. (Another *cathedral?* she would say with rolling eyes but a wry smile). Like many another non-believer I have no religious belief but recognise that these days there are few places left dedicated to peace, solitude and silence — specifically libraries, bookshops and ecclesiastical buildings and we saw plenty of all of them. (My quondam ambition to visit all the cathedrals in England got off to a relatively good start but faltered and now almost certainly will never be achieved. Without Rhona, why bother?). She did her thing; I did my thing; the most important thing is that we put up with each other's thing together. So many happy hours, captured on camera and in some cases video and now existing only in photographs, my diaries and in memories — mine alone. Diana Trilling, wife of the critic Lionel Trilling, wrote: "You know, the genius who invented marriage was inventing an extraordinary institution in which each of the two people is the most important person in the world to the other and this is something the closest friendship cannot provide." Nietzsche was right when he said that it isn't lack of love that makes for an unhappy marriage but lack of friendship.

As my relationship with Rhona deepened I found myself in at least some respects *in loco parentis* to David and Leah. This wasn't always especially easy; at the point of meeting Rhona I was only nine years older than her daughter and both of Rhona's children were at that time teenagers, already a difficult enough period for many youngsters without their added burden of having seen their father's long illness, sometimes erratic behaviour because of it and his brutally premature death. There were on occasion some fraught moments, no question, but on the whole we rubbed along well enough.

It was never a role I had seen myself occupying. Children had never figured in my life plan. In fact the very concept of having a life plan at all had never figured in my life; I seem to have bumbled and stumbled my way haphazardly through nearly half a century, most of the time only minimally aware of what I'm doing or supposed to be doing. Of course, more than twenty years my senior Rhona had done the parenthood thing twice. Nevertheless the idea of having children had decidedly never been on my radar so it was something of a surprise to say the least when, during our Stevenage years, Rhona and I had a brief pregnancy scare. I can't recall the year but some time in the late 1990s — or was it 2000? — Rhona missed a period (or several). She, or we, paid a visit to a local chemist for a pregnancy testing kit; Rhona duly pissed on the plastic stick as instructed and awaited the presence or the absence of a blue line in the tiny window. Minutes passed. Result: not pregnant. Of course, in hindsight and given her age a missed period was almost certainly the early indication of the onset of the sporadic periods that herald the beginning of the menopause (of which Rhona had a mercifully easy time, sailing through the process without the wearing problems that so many women experience); but for a short space it gave us pause. Would she have had a termination? We may well have talked about what we would do if she had been pregnant, though I don't now recall what conclusions we came to. We *might* have been parents — surprise babies are common enough and late forties babies are not wholly unknown — and it's sobering thought that had the blue line appeared in the window there's a possibility that, had we gone through with the pregnancy, our child would now be well into its twenties. But that was a road never taken. I don't regret this; one hostage to fortune is quite enough.

Chapter Five

Toy Goy

> The pursuit of knowledge for its own sake, an almost fanatical love of justice and the desire for personal independence—these are the features of the Jewish tradition which make me thank my lucky stars that I belong to it.
>
> —Albert Einstein: *The World As I See It*

Rhona was not, by even the most liberal interpretation of the word, a religious person; based on various comments made to me over the years she wavered between a tolerant, open-minded agnosticism — she respected religious belief in others without possessing it herself — and on other occasions a franker atheism. She had no belief in an afterlife. She may even have fought shy of the term 'spiritual'. (I have my own issues with the word too). And yet, for all that, she had no hesitation in regarding herself and calling herself Jewish since she was raised as such, however nominally; as a child she attended *cheder*, which can be thought of as a sort of Jewish equivalent to a Christian Sunday school where basic Jewish knowledge is imparted to the very young. Though she had no religion, if asked her religion or when required to fill in some official form for instance 'Jewish' was automatic. Orthodox Judaism accepts only matrilineal descent; that is to say, someone is born Jewish if and only if their mother is Jewish. For the Orthodox Jewish status is like mitochondrial DNA; it comes down the distaff side only. More liberal strands of Judaism accept someone as Jewish if either parent is Jewish, whereas the *really* liberal strands accept anybody as Jewish if they identify as such. By this yardstick Rhona was a Jew to everyone (albeit no doubt a bad one to the Orthodox). The way I've always put it to myself is that Judaism is a religion but Jewishness is an ethnicity, a culture and a sensibility — Rhona and I had many long, lively and involved discussions about this over the years. Jewishness in the ethnic, cultural rather than religious sense was always important to her; never obtrusive but important. It may have been noticeable to alert eyes — she regularly wore a Star of David pendant either around her neck or on a bracelet, for instance; we also had a mezuzah on the doorpost and a smallish menorah on the windowsill at the rear of the house, both bought on one of our regular visits to Golder's Green — but it was never overt and she was never religiously observant in the slightest. She had no time for the laws of *kashrut* (that is, keeping kosher), having no hesitation in regularly tucking into pork chops with apple sauce, bacon and shellfish — a prawn korma was a takeaway favourite; she avidly ate lobster whenever she could get it —, all of which are non-kosher foods and therefore absolutely forbidden to religiously observant Jews. She never set foot inside a *shul* (the Yiddish word for a synagogue) save for the Jewish analogues of hatching, matching and despatching (and bar mitzvahs). Perhaps I'm more of a black-and-white, all-or-nothing person than Rhona ever was; from time to time I used to quiz her on exactly how and in what sense she was Jewish if she followed precisely none of Judaism's rules and regulations. But I still maintain that Judaism and cultural Jewishness are two separate and discrete entities, and a Jewish sensibility informed so much of her life from beginning to end, and we come back to the concept of Jewishness as an ethnicity and culture rather than Judaism as a religion. Though devoutly secular, if asked of her she always identified as Jewish; it was as core an element of her being as was her name or her tastes in food. She was a mixture of the two great strands of European Jewry; her father Leslie's background was Ashkenazi (Eastern European) whereas that of her mother Zena was Sephardi (Mediterranean). Her conversation was occasionally peppered with the Yiddish words and phrases which she had heard while growing up; typically (or even stereotypically) Jewish food such as gefilte fish, chopped liver and chicken soup — all of which she made herself on a regular basis — and challah, the rich, sweet egg-glazed bread, were staples of her diet; she could (very) haltingly recall some Hebrew from her *cheder* days.

It was a sensibility which I adopted. Coming from a village in the heart of England Judaism and Jewishness were not exactly things which had previously featured on my intellectual radar. I knew precisely zero Jews — villages in rural Leicestershire tend not to have a Jewish community any more than they have a Chinatown — and no more than the average gentile's passing few facts about Judaism; so when I came to know that Rhona was Jewish (albeit nominally) I found an entirely new world opening up before me and from the off I was captivated. I am, I have to say, captivated still. Very early on in our relationship Rhona bought me a relatively cheap but attractive silver Star of David pendant on a silver chain from Stevenage indoor market which I put on then and have worn ever since — it hangs about my neck as I write and will continue to do so until a nurse or funeral director (presumably) removes it from my cooling corpse. In over twenty-one years it has been taken off, if I recall rightly, a grand total of three times, each time for dental or chest X-rays. Otherwise it has been a constant and will remain so. It's there for keeps.

It's frequently no easier to say why one becomes passionately attracted to a particular subject than it is to say why one falls passionately in love with a particular person. I know that I can't explain my love for, endless fascination with and absorption in Jewishness in rational terms; I can only say that it was akin in certain ways to another kind of falling in love; one of life's "aha!" moments, a sense of homecoming to a home I never even knew I yearned for. I was and am no more 'religious' in any tolerably conventional sense than was Rhona and by most would be thought to be considerably less, but the idea of Jewishness — *Yiddishkeit*; Jewishness as a marker of identity and culture, a certain view of and way of being in the world — rather than Judaism as a religion grabbed me at my core very early on and has, thank goodness, never let me go.

Inevitably I did what I invariably do when something grabs me and started to buy every book on the subject that spoke to me, laying out a good deal of money over time and eventually building up a rather impressive bookcase-full of which I'm still the proud guardian to this day since these are some of the most treasured books in what is a very large personal library. I taught myself some reasonable elegant biblical Hebrew (rusty and halting these days but fairly quickly revived) and racy, raunchy Yiddish (of which the late, great Leo Rosten said that it has more vitamins than other languages), one of the languages which I wish I could master completely. Though not religious I bought sundry handsomely-bound religious tomes the better to soak up Hebrew and to get inside the Jewish mind even if the religious Jewish mind; a *siddur* (Jewish prayer book), a *chumash* (the Torah or the first five books of what the gentile world calls the Old Testament) and a *tanakh* (the Old Testament in its entirety) amongst them; after so many years immersed in scripture if called upon I can, at least in principle, do sundry traditional Jewish prayers and blessings at the drop of a *yarmulke*. The by now well-worn *siddur* has rarely been out of my hands ever since; nobody has to take on all the tenets of Judaism-as-a-religion to find a wealth of profound wisdom and humane good sense in and to profit handsomely from the collection of sayings and teachings of ancient sages known as the *Pirkei Avot* (Ethics of the Fathers), for example. I read, studied and probed to the point where both Rhona and her brother Clive claimed, in all apparent seriousness, that through my own efforts, my own autodidactic course of study, I had come to know more about Judaism than they did. Not true but flattering nonetheless. I once came across the distinction made (by whom I don't know) of Jews-by-chance (that's to say those born Jewish if there can be such a thing, which in certain contexts I would dispute) and Jews-by-choice (those who willingly adopt a Jewish identity). If the distinction has any mileage in it Rhona — Jewish-by-chance — frequently said that I had learnt more about Jewishness than she had forgotten.

Living in Stevenage as we then did London was within easy reach and we made regular trips down the A1 into the great wen and to London's Jewish heartland of Golders Green, where we parked up the car in a side street somewhere off Golders Green Road, shopped for *challah*, bagels and gefilte fish and other traditional Jewish staples, ate falafel sandwiches at the Taboon café — heavy on the onion; still some of the most delicious food I've ever eaten outside of Rhona's cooking and memorable all these years later — and I, *yarmulke* perched atop my still hairy head, browsed for an age and bought up books by the bagful in the Menorah bookshop. Because I am dark and what some would consider to be florid-featured Rhona was much amused by the fact that I could apparently 'pass' as authentically Jewish in one of the capital's Jewish strongholds. In some ways I felt like an utter fraud, of course, but in other ways I was perfectly at home even amongst Orthodox Jews with the *tzitzit* (fringes) of their *talittot* (prayer shawls) dangling outside their clothing. In many ways this was a strange and alien world to me — not merely the world of London to this Leicestershire village boy but the world of religious Jewry — but it was a world which I had freely and willingly adopted as my own.

Years later, now moved back to Leicestershire, my adherence to Judaism awoke again. There is no specific Jewish area of Leicester as such as there is in London and Manchester to name but two British cities but I discovered that there is a very liberal progressive Jewish congregation in a leafy area of the city with a synagogue named Neve Shalom ('Oasis of Peace'). I made approaches, and one night Rhona and I attended a *seder* night for Passover (one of the most important Jewish festivals; possibly the most important of all) where I, like the rest of the congregation one by one, uncomfortably read out a small portion of the Passover *Haggadah* (in essence the 'script' for the *seder* night service). A little later I even looked into full conversion to Judaism; in a Leicester hotel one bright afternoon I had a lengthy meeting with Neve Shalom's then-rabbi, who quizzed me, as do all good rabbis, on my attachment to Judaism and my motivation in seeking to convert. Judaism is not a proselytising religion which actively seeks converts (though old tales of prospective converts being turned away three times before acceptance are just that — tales) and some rabbis are understandably somewhat wary of those who seek to convert because they are in a romantic relationship with someone Jewish; but had it not been for my relationship with Rhona I would never have had any reason to delve into Judaism and Jewishness as I did and would never have found the closest thing to a spiritual home that I have.

It went no further than that. I never did formally convert, which in some ways I regret to this day. In the end I didn't do so for several reasons. One is that I can't quite bring myself to believe in the concept of an all-knowing, all-seeing and above everything else all-good God — the world would be very much otherwise if such a thing existed. Take the classic example: the Holocaust. Now it's true that even some quite conservative Jewish authorities will tell you that Jewish practice is more important than belief and that a belief in God is, while not exactly optional, something for each individual to work out for themselves. Therefore, I reasoned, I would be converting not to Judaism as a religion but to a decidedly secular form of *Jewishness*, and that is surely open and available to one and all, myself included. I felt and feel that I was and am already Jew-ish — the hyphen is all-important. Secondly even under liberal Jewish auspices I would have to be circumcised, with which practice I profoundly disagree when performed on non-consenting babies. Fine for competent consenting adults who can choose it freely — difficult, painful and expensive as it is — but I do not, have never and will never agree that it is right to inflict unnecessary surgery on newborns in the name of religion or tradition. Not just newborns: I'm not enamoured of any club that requires surgery for one to join it. Thirdly, I've always been wary of confining myself to any one specific philosophy — it took me until the age of forty-three to join a political party, for example — and by nailing my colours to the mast of Jewish adherence I felt as though I would be ruling out (and missing out on) the various bits and pieces of wisdom to be gleaned from other religious traditions such as Hinduism, let's say, or Buddhism, or Jainism, or even paganism. So I didn't in the end convert, though even to this very day I don't entirely rule it out of court altogether; not because in the wake of Rhona's death I've undergone some kind of abrupt religious awakening

— that's definitely not the case — but because a commitment to Jewishness, becoming a Jew-by-choice, is a means, however vicarious, of maintaining a commitment to Rhona, a Jew-by-chance.

I am not a Jew and can't, don't and won't call myself such. I'm not able to, unfortunately. I wish I had that honour and that privilege, for an honour and a privilege it surely is. But I do consider myself to be Jew-ish. If there is such a thing as a Jew-ish soul I think, I believe, *I hope*, that I have it and understand it. This concept of Jew-ishness is explored in a wry and entertaining 2009 *Guardian* article by the (born Jewish) writer Jonathan Margolis:

> What I really want to write about is being Jew-*ish*. This is a term that I wish I'd invented rather than the veteran doctor-slash-theatre-producer, Jonathan Miller, years ago. He also referred to being "an amphibious Jew – half in and half out of the water."
>
> We are those cop-out, fair-weather Jews that "real" Jews despise more than they do anti-Semites: the secular, cultural Jews, the amoral majority, the ones who want to have their bagel and eat it. The ones who, with their marrying out, their going to the pub on Yom Kippur and to the football on Saturdays, and — God forbid — with their ambivalent view of the Middle East, are doing Hitler's work for him and conspiring in the erosion of the already disappearing UK Jewish community — currently about 250,000 and counting, downwards.
>
> Leaving aside what's supposed to be wrong with having your cake and eating it (what else are you supposed to do with a cake? Frame it? Bury it?), I can't help feeling the time has come for us race traitors, half-breeds and "apathites" to stand up for ourselves.

> Apart from the not insignificant point that being a Jew is largely an inherited condition, it seems perfectly adapted to being an "-ish" [...] There aren't many other things you can be born into where you can choose to live the "-ish" version rather than be an "-ist" or follow an "-ism". All we Jew-ish Jews do is to elect for the Ultra Lite option.
>
> For us, the cool thing about being born a Jew is that you can do it as much or as little, as well or as badly, as you like. You can be professional, amateur or pro-am. This understandably pisses off the pros, who marry a fellow full-timer, know all the stuff in the manual and keep up with all the latest fads [...]
>
> Jew-ish is different, you see, from lapsed. You can't lapse from being a Jew like you can from other things. Plenty of German Jews in the 1930s thought that simply saying they were no longer interested would get them off the hook with the Nazis; it didn't. And we, the Jew-ish, have no wish to deny our heritage [...]

Rhona called herself Jewish and was proud to do so; furthermore, when asked (such as on official forms for example) what her religion (if any) was, she consistently wrote 'Jewish' (which annoyed me a little since she practiced no religion). That said, she barely even did the Ultra Lite option; in her case it was vegan, decaffeinated, low-sodium, gluten-free diet Jewishness with no added religion, and even then predominantly when it came to food.

In spite of everything, for good or bad, because of Rhona I stand with the Jewish people in most things. By no means all things; I am not a Jew and have serious disagreements with some of the core elements of Judaism-as-a-religion. I don't stand with Israel in everything. Nevertheless, from the first day to this I had and have a lover's quarrel with Judaism or rather Jew-ishness. With Ruth I say: do not entreat me to turn aside, for their people are my people; wherever they go, I go; and their God (whatever God may be) is my God. I'm not at all sure about the last bit — I'm still working on that — but the rest can stand.

Chapter Six

Moving On

> For the two of us, home isn't a place. It is a person. And we are finally home.
>
> —Stephanie Perkins: *Anna and the French Kiss*

Rhona had landed in Stevenage as a result of John's work and the need (or desire) to be able to commute to the capital but not to live there, but after his death and as the children were growing toward adulthood she began to wonder, frequently aloud, what was still tying her to the town and whether she wanted to continue to live there and if so, for what reason. John was and is buried there, of course, but Rhona — unlike me, brought up on it on an almost weekly basis — had never understood (and moreover was frankly baffled by) the practice of visiting the graves of loved ones or why people feel the need to do so. By and by — I don't remember the discussions; it's so long ago — Rhona and I agreed that with Leah heading out in the grown-up world of work and David rapidly approaching the end of his days of education, we would up sticks and move to my home county of Leicestershire, possibly (and hopefully) to somewhere a little more rural, greener and less urban. Rhona, who had grown up in the north-east, had lived in London for several years and had spent twenty years in Stevenage, regularly used to say that she could make a nest anywhere, but to head eighty miles north to relocate to a county she didn't know was a considerable sacrifice on her part. To me it was in effect a move back home; it was as much of a leap into the dark for Rhona as my move to Stevenage had been for me almost three years earlier. But that was what we chose to do.

Through much of the year 2000 we made many a journey up and down the motorway between Stevenage and various locations in Leicestershire while we were house-hunting, of which we did a great deal. Sometimes one of us fell in love with a house that the other one hated; sometimes we both rejected a particular property; in one specific case we both fell in love with a sizeable house in my home village of Earl Shilton, not so far from my parents (and even closer to my former local), only to be gazumped at almost the last moment.

Finally, after viewing more properties than I can possibly remember, we found The One; a late 1960s three-bedroomed semi-detached house with a large Norway maple outside (adorned in spring and summer with leathery, wine-red leaves), last-but-one at the end of a quiet cul-de-sac called Wareham Road on what was then the very edge — no longer so — of the large village (or small town) of Blaby, about five miles from the centre of Leicester (some eight or so miles from Earl Shilton) and within budget. This was and is the heart of suburbia, populated predominantly by middle-class and at the very least middle-aged couples; CaravanLand as Rhona and I mischievously called it. We viewed the property and more or less instantly decided that this would be our new home, not least because for me at that time the end of the cul-de-sac gave out onto a large, open field and beyond that a nine-hole golf course. (I say 'at that time' because subsequently, to my rage, disappointment and disgust, it has been obliterated by a housing estate). It wasn't exactly the rural idyll that I'd dreamed of (nor Rhona, a townie to the core and for which we didn't have the budget anyway) but it was the next best thing. I compromised on that while Rhona compromised on the huge kitchen that she would have liked. I wouldn't care to stretch the analogy too far but finding the right home is a little like finding the right partner in life; when you know, you simply *know*. The chemistry is right; there is the feeling of all the pieces slotting into their proper place.

On one particular sunny day some time in 2000 we made the journey from Stevenage to Blaby in order to view the house again and possibly with shop-bought sandwiches we had an improvised picnic in the field and decided that this was perfection — or at least as close to it as we were likely to get. It wasn't my rose-bedecked cottage in the country but I compromised on that; it had only an average-sized kitchen but Rhona compromised on that. It was simply right for the both of us. An offer was made; was accepted; and we set about the process of decamping from the home counties to the Midlands.

We made the move in mid-November 2000. I left Stevenage with some sadness; I am, I freely admit, the most fearfully sentimental of men (I keep train tickets and even till receipts as mementos of where I've been and when, useful when you keep a diary) and had grown attached even to the urban sprawl of the first post-war new town. I — we — had been happy there. It had been where my relationship with Rhona had begun and had almost instantly blossomed into the first and only truly serious long-term committed relationship of my life; that single factor alone made and still makes Stevenage somewhere special to me. But we were heading north to my home shire (though not to especially familiar territory even to me let alone Rhona; though only a few miles from Earl Shilton I didn't know Blaby) and to a nice house in a nice street in a nice village. My parents' moving-in gift to us both was an expensive king-sized divan bed of a kind not too often made these days, I think; with a brass bedstead and a phenomenally heavy mattress, the whole thing weighing a quarter of a ton or so it seemed. With my mum pitching in with a paintbrush we started decorating on the same day that we took possession of the keys on the Saturday that we moved in, November 18th 2000.

Short of one day it would remain our home for the next eighteen years.

Chapter Seven

Dulce Domum

Home is where the heart is.

—Proverb

Leah, now working, stayed behind in Stevenage whereas David came with us to Leicestershire until his move to the US several years later. I had been aware (although not uncomfortably so) that in moving to Archer Road I had moved into the home that Rhona had shared with John for many years — and in which he had died, of course — and partly in which David and Leah had been raised; now, however, Wareham Road was ours, a fresh start and a new beginning of sorts. Never one for looking back as I have always been, Rhona set about creating her new nest. Although Rhona was not, unlike me, notably an animal lover, in time we acquired from the local animal shelter a fat, eight year-old black and white cat ('tuxedo' as the Americans say) called Tansy — the first of a succession of felines — and later a Cavalier King Charles Spaniel called Susie. Both of us had been brought up with dogs (Cavaliers in Rhona's case, hence the choice of breed) but now I became the full-time dogfather; living next to nearly eight acres of open greenery I walked Susie two, three, four times a day, spending uncountable hours ambling around the field and across the golf course in all weathers — scorching heatwaves, pelting rain, hail, nearly up to my knees in snow. Neither Rhona or I were keen or even knowledgeable gardeners; all we knew is that in the spring and summer months we liked a multitude of pots, tubs and troughs in the small back garden (big enough for the pair of us and easy to take care of) filled with masses of colourful blooms, and each spring we bought huge bags of compost and trays of plants and spent many a happy hour outside potting up in preparation for the random riot of colour we enjoyed in summer.

Despite being only eight or nine miles or so from Earl Shilton where I grew up I hadn't been familiar with Blaby and its environs prior to moving there. Like Earl Shilton, Blaby hovers somewhere in the murky territory between being a large village or a small town; the Sorites paradox says that there are unambiguous villages and equally unambiguous towns but it's often difficult or even impossible to tell exactly where the former turns into the latter. Blaby is a bustling and, to me, bright, welcoming and friendly little place, divided (as Earl Shilton is not) between the small red-brick cottages and narrow streets of old Blaby and street after street of the more spacious estates of new Blaby.

Amongst many other things Rhona and I shared a geekish love of maps; Rhona quickly acquainted herself with the area in which we now found ourselves. A sizeable chunk of largely rural (and extremely beautiful) central-southern Leicestershire now became our stamping ground; where we worked, where we shopped, where we ate, where we drove simply for the pleasure of it. This patch very roughly had Blaby in the north; Carlton Curlieu and Tur Langton in the east; Lutterworth in the south and Stoke Golding in the west. Along with the countryside surrounding Earl Shilton this, to me, is *echt* Leicestershire; wide expanses of farmland dotted with sheep and cows, undulating fields, quiet lanes frothing in summer with honeysuckle and cow parsley, chocolate box villages. If ever I wavered in my belief that we lived a blessed life — not that I did or was ever likely to — a quick tootle out in the car confirmed it. At the other end of the spectrum Blaby is just five miles south from the centre of Leicester, separated from the city's southernmost suburb (Glen Parva) only by a single field, so trips into the city were easy and frequent. Fosse Park, Meridian and Grove

Farm Triangle, major retail parks just outside of Leicester, were a few miles away; and by sheer but happy coincidence, as well as the two superstores in Blaby itself we found ourselves within a few miles in every direction of all the major supermarkets, offering Rhona endless shopping opportunities. Could things be any better?

In an account such as this it strikes me that it's a relatively straightforward matter to write about the bigger things in life — the triumphs and disasters, the great joys and great tragedies, the births, marriages and deaths, the significant stand-out events; to me it seems considerably more difficult to write about the ordinary, pedestrian, even humdrum daily pulse of everyday life for two people sharing just about everything every single day, day after day after day after day. If Rhona and I had been famous or had had lives packed full of great excitement, drama and incident it would be comparatively easy to provide an account of how our years together passed, but what does one say about the everyday life of two people living quietly and happily together in a largely unchanging household for over two decades? This is the sort of thing better fitted to a diary — such as the one I've kept almost daily since the age of eleven in October 1983 — rather than a memoir, since diaries by definition catch some of the ebb and flow of everyday life. (Beginning in her adolescence Rhona had herself been an assiduous diary keeper but gave it up around the time of her marriage; later attempts were rare, desultory and quickly abandoned). While just about everything we did — the places we went to; even what we ate — found its way into the diary, a settled, orderly, happy life doesn't translate so well to the pages of a memoir. It's not easy to write about the mundanities of day-in, day-out life, especially a quiet and home-centred life such as we always led. Experienced journalists, who can live up to the stereotype of being a cynical, hard-bitten bunch, know that bad news sells whereas good news doesn't; there's no copy to be had in a quiet, peaceful, simple and happy life. Rhona and I were together — Team Wowo as Rhona sometimes put it — for a few weeks shy of twenty-one years and for me at least away from the diary there's no obvious way to encapsulate such a lengthy stretch of time on a day-by-day basis. *What are days for?* as Philip Larkin famously asked and immediately answered his own question: days are where we live; they are to be happy in. For twenty-one years, in Stevenage and then in Blaby, Rhona and I did what everybody else does in this world: we lived out our days a day at a time. A quiet life; a mundane, humdrum, even boring life to some no doubt; but nevertheless it was our life. Not just the big things but the little, the littlest things, the daily routines of ordinary people living an ordinary life, are the bricks, the most elementary of particles of which marriages are built, something captured by Jonathan Santlofer in *The Widower's Notebook*: "When I think about it, I'd say that what I came to miss most were the ordinary moments of our daily life, the in-between stuff when you don't know anything is happening, the infinite forgettable moments." In *Anne of Avonlea* L. M. Montgomery had expressed much the same sentiment: "I believe the nicest and sweetest days are not those on which anything very splendid or wonderful or exciting happens but just those that bring simple little pleasures, following one another softly, like pearls slipping off a string."

One of the things that I loved most about our home life first in Stevenage and then in Blaby was its permanence. Everybody is different, everybody is an individual ("*I'm not*" says that little man in *Life of Brian*) but I am the sort of person or personality who dislikes, distrusts, even hates and fears too much change too quickly. Some people thrive on it but I've never handled change well. Life in Blaby provided me with the sort of stability and continuity — perhaps even predictability, though for most people (not me) that's not usually thought of as a positive term — that comes naturally to me. I don't know whether it was through sheer inertia or whether Rhona felt the same way about it but our home was in some ways akin to a time capsule; decidedly not that it was old-fashioned, stuck in this or that era, but rather that over the years our home changed little and changed very slowly. Certainly we had new carpets, new furniture, new decoration, new appliances, alterations from time to time; but these were relatively rare exceptions. Generally speaking when something was put in place it stayed there unmoved, often for years at a time, as innumerable photographs attest where you can see the same ornaments and decorations in situ year after year after year.

In twenty-one years Rhona and I spent almost all of our time together in a way which I think is unusual for the vast majority of couples, leading what would be seen by many no doubt as a cloistered, insular existence. I should say that even today, with most couples one (or increasingly both) go out to work in the morning and come home again at night, several hours later, having been apart in the interim, chatting about their respective days over dinner. For us it was different. John's death had left Rhona reasonably financially secure thanks in large part to a generous BT pension and a life insurance policy — scant recompense for losing your spouse aged only forty after five harrowing years of illness but initially with a teenaged daughter and adolescent son it was Rhona's fiscal lifeline. Because neither of us initially worked (or later on, when we did so, it was largely working at home at things that we could do together) this was never the case for us; we spent almost all our time in each other's company day and night, again to a degree far beyond that of the vast majority of couples. We slept next to each other at night, yes, but spent the bulk of our daylight hours together as well. We were … *unusually* together. In so many respects we were blessed with, until what turned out to be the end, a charmed life. Due to my mental health issues I lived precariously on what was in those days known as incapacity benefit; Rhona subsisted on John's life insurance and pensions; later on she would become involved in the world of organising beauty pageants and, later still, would become an avid and extremely successful seller on eBay, making her the main breadwinner. We never had a conventional relationship (whatever that may be, especially these days), not only in terms of age but in terms of finances. Freed from the daily grind of having to go out to work we spent our days pursuing whatever took our fancy. I'm as much of a home body and nest-builder as Rhona ever was and was an assiduous house husband, rarely happier than when taking over the daily business of looking after a comparatively sizeable home; the vacuuming, the dusting, the polishing, the window cleaning, emptying and refilling the dishwasher, putting the bins out, even — though I don't claim to be any kind of specialist and certainly have some major blind spots such as electrics, which I won't touch — some of the DIY. At one point during our three years in Stevenage we decided to revamp the kitchen and I, with enormous care and great physical effort, spent considerable time retiling it in handsome (albeit thick and heavy) hand-made Victorian green tiles with floral tacos in between. And rather a good job I made of it if I say so myself. (A subsequent visit to Stevenage a few years after we left and a surreptitious look at the old house over the garden fence revealed that the new owners, not finding the tiles to their taste, had ripped them out). Rhona went abroad on a number of occasions, variously to Florida to see David and his family or latterly to accompany her mum on luxury cruises; apart from our very early week in Tunisia — my first and only venture abroad — foreign travel was beyond me, but we travelled extensively around many parts of England, sometimes for Rhona's work-related reasons, sometimes for the sheer pleasure of it.

Though we spent far, far, far more time in each other's company than the vast majority of couples, the fact that we maintained separate interests meant that our relationship never felt claustrophobic or cloying. We shared far more interests and had much more in common than the reverse, but for all that there were things that Rhona was interested in and pursued in which I wasn't particularly interested and vice versa. I think that this is not merely healthy but vital in any successful union; it's one of the things that prevents each half of a couple from being a mere mirror of the other.

The old stereotypical joke is that Jewish mothers are travel agents for guilt trips. The equally old and in this case (in my experience) less stereotypical joke is that Jewish mothers are great 'feeders' — wanting to feed everybody and anybody to a sufficiency and beyond, for whom the immediate answer to any and every of life's problems is to *fress* (that is, in Yiddish, to eat). A good *nosh* is an essentially Jewish (again a specifically Yiddish, linguistically) thing. Don't get me wrong: until dialysis robbed us of Saturday evenings together we enjoyed a Saturday night takeaway as much as anybody else (by my preference Chinese food, which I could and can eat endlessly; the occasional curry — prawn korma for Wo; vegetable jalfrezi for me — and an even rarer pizza) but proper home-made, home-cooked food was one of our greatest passions. We were not gluttons; Rhona loved cooking as do I but at points in my life, with so many millions of people in the world going hungry and even starving to death daily, I've often found it hard to justify the love, care and attention of a very privileged minority in a relatively small part of the planet lavished upon food. Nevertheless; food — good food and lots of it —, whether freshly cooked at home or eaten out, played a huge part in our lives. At home I had been raised on doubtless nutritious but stodgy and stereotypically English fare, a traditional meat-and-potatoes diet of overcooked vegetables and watery gravy bordering on the bland. In the 1980s sashimi, black olives, kimchi, couscous or sun-dried tomatoes were a very, very, *very* long way away indeed from a village such as Earl Shilton in terms of time let alone physical distance. If asked merely to try something such as, for example, squid, most inhabitants would have looked as you as though you had invited them to eat their own legs from the feet upwards. By adulthood I had started to break away from the, I have to say, uninspired diet of my early years and had begun to expand my palate considerably; but Rhona, older, well-travelled and quite cosmopolitan as she was, introduced me to a planet's worth of exotic dishes not to be found in Earl Shilton — classic Jewish cuisine; traditional middle-eastern foods such as *foul medames* (a fairly regular treat for us both; cooked broad or fava beans served in pitta bread or wraps with judiciously-applied coriander, cumin, olive oil, lemon juice and chopped raw red onion) which she had picked up from her several trips to Egypt. Rhona had a life-long aversion to spicy food and couldn't tolerate more than the most timid amount of chilli in any dish, yet we ate out often and ate our way around the world. Chinese. Indian. French. Italian. Greek. Turkish. Lebanese. Thai. Japanese — name it and we ate it. Although we loved a 'posh' restaurant as much as any food critic, we weren't above a weekly curry (in Stevenage Old Town especially) or an all-you-can-eat pig-out buffet. Rhona loved food and was in every sense a natural feeder; her Jewish background made food — shopping; choosing; preparing; cooking; serving; entertaining; eating — a central element in our lives together. When we moved from Hertfordshire to Leicestershire in 2000 the number one item on Rhona's wish list for her new home was a huge kitchen; big enough not only for a really good cooker, all the pots and pans and other utensils, an island perhaps, but comfy couches for people to sit on and chat while she cooked and even a TV. We didn't get that — we both had to compromise on our wishes on the basis of budget — but within our means we ended up with a kitchen that still spoke to Rhona's marrow-deep love of cooking and entertaining.

Like many women (and, I'm told, increasingly some men) Rhona had a complex and sometimes not always healthy relationship with food and with eating, particularly in her early life. In her younger days she struggled with her weight to the extent that when she reached twenty-three stones, at the age of twenty-three she underwent, in Birmingham in 1974, a massive operation involving the resection and bypassing of a large portion of her intestine (surgery now no longer performed, so I understand, since subsequent research has indicated that in later life it can lead to vitamin deficiencies and even arthritis), which leads to permanent and constant diarrhoea. She was never as hefty as that again; but despite this, until she became ill Rhona was a big lady, as innumerable photographs attest. She ate well, cooked fantastically well, entertained well. Rhona was a superb cook; while filial loyalty demands of me that I'm supposed to say that my mum was the best cook I've ever known, the truth is that Rhona was her match in most respects and in many respects her superior, in technical skill and especially in variety. As well as deliberating over this and that in a supermarket she was at her happiest in the kitchen, chopping and peeling and stirring, standing over a hot pan on the hob with a spoon or a ladle. Especially first thing in the morning, when we were both up and eating breakfast, we were almost slavishly devoted to the food channels on satellite TV such as The Food Network — programmes such as *Barefoot Contessa*, *The Pioneer Woman* and anything with Jamie Oliver; several bookshelves groaned, bowed down (and literally, as in literally curved) with hefty cookery books. Rhona's thick, piping hot leek and potato soup, regularly made, was to die for; likewise with her oozy, unctuous cauliflower cheese, topped variously with tomatoes or mushrooms. Mushrooms were a favourite; Rhona's rich, creamy mushroom soup and her silky mushroom risotto, cooked to perfection, had to be tasted to be believed. Then there was her claggy but delicious potato salad. Classic Jewish food was very much to the fore; holikshes (cabbage leaves stuffed with meat and rice); her chicken soup — the archetypical cure-all 'Jewish penicillin', with vermicelli noodles — was in our house the stuff of legend, something that she made regularly for herself and sometimes others and something that, despite being a long-standing vegetarian, I diligently made for her whenever she was under the weather. Jewish vegetarianism is more than common enough these days but traditional Ashkenazi cooking tends to be heavy on meat and fish (and to be fair but frank, simply heavy full stop) — and as a vegetarian from the age of about twenty-one there were a number of regularly-made dishes which were denied to me; the already mentioned chicken soup being one, her garlic-laced chopped liver on matzos being another. That said, one of her many specialities was another Jewish classic, gefilte fish; little balls of mixed and finely-chopped fish bound together with egg and matzo meal, variously fried (according to some cookbooks the English way and the best way in my opinion; done right, crisp and crunchy on the outside, soft and moist on the inside) and/or traditionally boiled, in the latter case topped with a sliver of sliced carrot — comparatively expensive, arduous, fiddly, time-consuming and pretty smelly to make, which is why it was only an occasional treat, but utterly delightful. By the time that Rhona and I met I had been a committed vegetarian for several years and therefore by definition not supposed to be a fish eater; but I have to put my hands up and admit that on these rare occasions even I lapsed, straying from the straight and narrow path of vegetarian purity and falling prey to the temptation of these small mouthfuls of delicious gorgeousness which Rhona made from time to time when she was in the mood to buy a large amount of fish, blitzed in the food processor with egg and matzo meal and then, as before, fried or boiled. When we moved to Leicestershire we acquired a deep-fat fryer and it fell to me to stand guard with my tongs and layers of kitchen roll over the seething boiling oil — in the garage, to keep the small of fish out of the house. Rhona loved to entertain friends and family and was (amongst other things such as shopping) at her happiest spending hours in the kitchen preparing and serving a lavish dining table's worth of delicious food. Rhona's ideal, Jewish as she was, was what she always thought of as the stereotypical

Italian family meal; lots of family gathered noisily around a large table, everybody picking at this or that dish as takes their fancy. I was less sold on this aspect of things; I'm not gregarious and as an introvert am not a naturally sociable man — I'm not, never have been and never will be a people person as Rhona, though decidedly not an extravert, absolutely was — and I admit that I found the human interaction side of this sort of thing a bit of a trial at times. But nobody would have been able to argue that the spread laid out on the table before them on the extendable dining table was anything other than splendid, and that's putting it mildly. Full-to-bursting cupboards, full-to-bursting freezers, a groaning dining table was in so many ways Rhona the feeder, Rhona the home body, Rhona the earth mother, Rhona the nest-builder, at the top of her form. I was a big eater too in those days; already carrying a few more pounds than I should have been (according to doctors, and doctors as we know is all swabs), when we met Rhona's delicious cooking added still more timber to my ample frame — though not carrying the full-on bay window, photos of me at this time reveal a decided spare tyre. Rhona did the bulk of the cooking until she became ill, at which point I took over a larger share of kitchen duty. Year in and year out she cooked for me, I cooked for her, but some of my happiest memories of our years in Blaby are of hours spent together in the relatively small but well-stocked kitchen assembling this or that dish. The soups already mentioned; a colossal mash-topped fish pie; a vegetable lasagne fit to feed a medium-sized central European republic; roasted vegetables laced with garlic and drenched in olive oil and balsamic vinegar; cauliflower cheese; mushroom risotto. I wasn't exactly a stranger to the kitchen myself; without wishing to blow my own bugle, when I was twenty, during a brief spell of unemployment, I cast around for something with which to fill my hours and for reasons now lost to me I hit upon learning to cook. Delia Smith's copper-bottomed classic *Complete Cookery Course* was a gentle and easy introduction to this venture — not to a professional standard of course but good, honest, tasty and attractive, broadly European cooking which stood me in good stead in times to come not only in looking after myself whenever I needed to but especially in looking after Rhona much, much later when she was too ill and too tired and debilitated to cook for herself.

My mum, to whom I was devoted, didn't have long to see Rhona and me happily settled in our lovely new home. With my dad and aunt Joan she was a frequent visitor to Wareham Road; but at the end of July 2001, only a few months after retirement from her job as a cook in a home for the elderly, she came down with what initially seemed like a mild illness no worse than a cold. In actual fact it turned out to be diverticulitis which, untreated, perforated her intestine and led in a matter of days to sepsis — even now a grave medical emergency. Within not much more than two weeks in Leicester Royal Infirmary's intensive care unit, a little after 9:00am on August 8th of that year she was dead at sixty-three. Rhona and I were present at the time, along with my dad and my aunt Joan. Rhona would be my rock during the grief that ensued. It was the first death I had personally witnessed, at my mum's bedside, holding her hand.

It would not be the last.

At the age of twenty-nine the loss of my mum so suddenly was the greatest blow in my life to that point. I know that in the most immediate aftermath I was in a state of shock and denial, because I have a particularly vivid memory of being driven from Leicester Royal Infirmary back to Earl Shilton and doing what I always did with any significant news; thinking *Good God, mum's just died; I must ring her and tell her.* I was absolutely shattered by it and without wishing to adopt an air of melodrama I consider it one of those kinds of losses that one never entirely 'gets over'. In fact I've learnt the hard way that however kindly meant it may be when other people say it 'getting over' a bereavement is not a phrase that should ever be deployed and is, as far as I'm concerned, long overdue for retirement.

In early July 2011, at the Greyhound Inn in the nearby town of Lutterworth, Rhona celebrated her 60th birthday at what she called on the invitations her 'I Can't Believe I Made It To 60' party. Rhona — Rhona, the free-wheeling, easy-riding, Isle-of-Wight-festival, acid-dropping hippy — never expected to see sixty, and yet here she was, surrounded by the people who loved her. Friends and family came from far and wide to celebrate Rhona's special day, complete with gigantic cake. I'm not in any of the photographs of this wonderful day — I was behind the lens, taking them.

There were less happy occasions, of course. Rhona experienced her own losses, principally that of her beloved dad Leslie in June 2010, ill with various conditions for several years prior but dying suddenly and peacefully within a matter of hours following a routine visit to the GP. And yet, tragedies such as these to one side for the moment, life in Blaby was good to us and for us for many long, happy, placid, outwardly uneventful years. Whether you think of it as a very large village or a small town I found, and find, it a cheery, active, attractive place, well served by shops but with quiet green areas too. In our eighteen years in Blaby there's scarcely a shop that Rhona and I didn't visit at least once or a street that we didn't drive down. On occasion I used to stop and catch myself thinking "Exactly *how* did I end up here?" — though a mere eight or so miles from Earl Shilton, Blaby wasn't a place I had known at all well prior to actually moving there, having never done more than pass through it on a few occasions on the way to somewhere else. Nevertheless it became, simply *was*, home; and even though I don't live there anymore, in some sense it will always be home. I live elsewhere now and may for as much as I know end up living somewhere else entirely again; but Blaby will always be home to me, with all that that word entails. It was where Rhona and I lived and loved — and yes, argued, split up, cried too. But it was where we were for eighteen years and the place that after a brief separation (more of which anon) I came back to when in due course Rhona's health broke down. To me the not being there can never be anything other than a form of (presumably; it's not likely that I'll ever go back) permanent internal exile. I hope that I'm sufficiently self-aware to realise that to others there may be something faintly ridiculous in waxing lyrical about a large and perhaps to those same others nondescript and perhaps even ordinary village in central Leicestershire rather than some glorious, glamorous spot in Provence or Tuscany; truth be told, my view is that there is never anything ridiculous in waxing lyrical about wherever your heart belongs. I may live in this or that particular spot but away from Blaby and our nest in Wareham

Road I have no home in the fullest, truest sense of that word and am for ever uprooted, for ever in exile from the place where I felt and feel (and expect always to feel) that I truly belong. I have learnt the hard way that home and where you happen to live (especially when forced to) are two entirely separate and discrete concepts. I miss Blaby dreadfully and long to see it again; to walk its so familiar streets, to shop in its so familiar shops, perhaps to run into someone I may know who will be too polite to say how much weight I've lost and how grey and untidy my beard has become. I sit and write only eight or so miles from it; yet it may as well be on the other side of the solar system. I miss it horribly, think of it often and yearn to go back there; but nearly ten months after Rhona's death and only five months after leaving it I know that the experience would be too raw, too sickeningly painful. Maybe one day … maybe, maybe not. Because of Rhona — solely because of Rhona — my heart belongs there. In *Night Train to Lisbon* Pascal Mercier wrote: "We leave something of ourselves behind when we leave a place, we stay there, even when we go away. And there are things in us that we can find again only by going back there." For all that we endured the inevitable difficult times, my memories of our eighteen years in Blaby are almost entirely happy and beautiful ones; but for that very reason, without Rhona, right now all that awaits me there is pain. Again, that may change, it may not. I don't envision putting it to the acid test of experience any time soon.

The days, the weeks, the months, the years passed. To my dismay it feels as though I'm skipping over a very long period of time and a great deal of life in a superficial and cursory manner; but Rhona and I lived a largely uneventful life, warm, cosy, happy and loving though it was. As I've already said this sort of fairly small, contented life isn't easy to write about; without drama and grand events there's not much in the way of a story in two happy people living a placid, home-centred life. We lived like any other perfectly ordinary couple. We shopped most days; we cooked; we ate handsomely at home and out of it; we watched TV and listened to music and read books; we had long and involved conversations about items of news and current affairs that piqued our interest (or indeed about almost anything and everything under the sun);

we laughed; we cried; we argued; we wrapped parcels and took them to the post office; we swapped funny stories and had our look-at-each-other-knowingly-without-saying-anything in-jokes; we used pet names for each other; we lived; we loved.

In short, we shared a happy life together in our beautiful home in a quiet street for very close to eighteen years. I don't pretend to understand or to explain it but I think there's little doubt that some people are more sensitive to what we can call 'atmosphere' than others; a friend of ours, on paying her first visit to our house, remarked on how warm and happy a home it felt. It all seems a bit New Agey but as I say, I don't know what sort of vibe people pick up on or even if there's anything to this but there's no doubt that she was absolutely right.

Through a common friend Rhona became involved in the world of beauty pageants, eventually becoming so knowledgeable that she organised her own heats (predominantly in Hertfordshire and Bedfordshire; some other counties as well, occasionally) for the Miss England contest. I know that beauty pageants get a bad rap from some quarters, being seen as old-fashioned at best, possibly shallow and politically incorrect, according to some even demeaning at worst, but I think that such criticisms are misguided and uninformed. Nobody is forced into them — it's not as though it's arms dealing or the white slave trade. Call me a cynic but the attitude of some feminists critical of beauty pageants (which are by no means solely about physical attractiveness any more) seems to be that women should be free to make their own choices and direct the course of their own lives provided that they make their choices from a carefully approved shortlist — carefully approved by them, needless to say. I've seen at first hand that many young highly intelligent, accomplished and ambitious young women love taking part and it was work that Rhona enjoyed immensely and threw herself into with her customary gusto for many years. To top up the income each year Rhona and I would also organise the delivery of telephone books and other directories — Yellow Pages; Thomson Local; Business Pages and the like — to bring in extra money in time for Christmas. The preparation for this involved a great deal of paperwork and the creation of maps for routes, something we could do together at our large dining table. More enjoyably for me it also involved travelling around great swathes of largely rural Leicestershire. Later on she discovered the joys of eBay and became an expert eBayer, something she could do stationary on the bed or on the couch with her beloved iPad when her health was fragile and her mobility impaired.

My health wasn't quite all that it could have been, either psychologically or physically. In the autumn of 2015 what seemed to be a three-week-long bout of the worst case of flu ever revealed me to be borderline dangerously anaemic; I had lost a large volume of blood due to a bleeding peptic ulcer which put me into Leicester Royal Infirmary for a few days and half a dozen blood transfusions. This flared up again almost exactly two years later when I had a second episode of ejecting tarry, Bible-black blood from both ends (at one point simultaneously, which is a novel experience if nothing else). Worst of all and with the most enduring consequences for the both is us, beginning in May 2003 and lasting for several months I endured what I can only call, for want of a far better phrase, a catastrophic nervous breakdown from the effects of which I've never entirely recovered. It took the form not, as in pre-Rhona years, of depression but disabling anxiety and panic attacks, presenting itself as a severe case of agoraphobia which has never entirely left me. Even now, nearly seventeen years later, I've never fully got over it and still can't travel easily (and certainly not with complete strangers) without tranquilisers. For a couple who spent an unusual amount of time together this put a considerable degree of strain on the relationship, partly for Rhona and partly on my part on Rhona's behalf. It wasn't my fault and yet I still felt — and feel — that I let her down somehow.

Rhona didn't escape. In 2013 she had a temporary but at the time anxiety-inducing health scare (which, thank goodness, turned out to be a false alarm) when a routine blood test discovered unusual proteins in her blood indicative of MGUS — monoclonal gammopathy of unknown (or uncertain; or undetermined — take your pick) significance, not in itself cancer but a pre-cancerous condition which can in a minority of cases lead on to myeloma. Unlike myeloma MGUS itself is typically harmless, doesn't often cause any overt symptoms (or at least beyond numbness and tingling in the extremities) and doesn't require any treatment but needs to be monitored at relatively regular intervals ('watchful waiting') since as noted it can for some people be a precursor to myeloma; a 2009 study determined that almost all patients with myeloma had previously had MGUS but only around 10% of patients with MGUS went on the develop myeloma. For several months Rhona was monitored with intermittent blood tests to see if the MGUS was likely to develop into myeloma and on one occasion went through a, to me gruesome, bone marrow test involving the insertion of a needle into her hip; I was by her side and holding her hand as usual but studiously looking anywhere but at the business end; it was something which I would never have put myself through in a million years but Rhona, always vastly physically more courageous than I've ever been or ever will be — in medical matters especially —, submitted to it with good grace (although judicious use of gas and air helped). With the odds on her side one day we went to Leicester Royal Infirmary for the results of recent tests and were told that Rhona didn't have myeloma. The relief after such a long period of anxiety can hardly be described. This required no treatment of any kind, only occasional monitoring. Rhona had dodged a bullet and remained healthy. This would not always be the case, or for long.

Chapter Eight

There and Back Again

> A selfish person can still love someone else, can't they? Even when they've hurt them and let them down.
>
> —Rosamund Lupton: *Sister*

This is going to be difficult.

Beginning in mid-2011 I made the single greatest mistake of my life; I began a brief but initially torrid affair with a woman I had met online. The sexual component was highly charged but short-lived, lasting barely a couple of months; after that period she met the man that she would go on to marry and for the next eighteen months or so we conducted a purely platonic friendship — going out for meals, for drinks, remaining emotionally available for each other but having no further carnal component to our relationship.

It would be discourteous and ungallant of me to go into too much detail about this; names, dates, places, times, experiences. I have no desire to insult or impugn the lady in question by saying that I wish it had never happened; and yet, for all that, it was the single biggest error of my lifetime on the basis of the deep pain and the raging anger that it caused Rhona when she came to find out about the affair which she did in November 2014 (when it was long since done with and I had had no contact with the other lady for well over two years, I might add). There are no excuses here; there is no justification whatever for the thoughtlessness and selfishness I exhibited in embarking upon this liaison however brief it may have been. Nothing justifies, ever *could* justify, the hurt, the outrage, the sense of betrayal which I inflicted upon Rhona. My head was turned and I was weak. Somehow I forgot — temporarily — how lucky I had been and was. All I can say by way of an attempt at partial explanation (not, I hope, self-serving excuse) is that after fourteen years together Rhona and I had perhaps come to take each other for granted; we had been together so much, so constantly, for so long that we had started to overlook each other to an extent. It may be that a degree of this is almost inevitable in any marriage without extremely hard work day in and day out. All affairs are founded on the belief that the grass is greener on the other side of the fence, which is almost always an arrant delusion. The hurt that my disloyalty caused Rhona and the shame and the guilt which this causes me will stay with me to the day of my own death. And yet, as Joyce Carol Oates writes in *A Widow's Story*, "There is no purpose to a memoir, if it isn't honest." Honesty demands *all* the cards on the table, not just the best hand. In November 2014, for reasons that I'll gloss over, Rhona suddenly became aware of the affair and threw me out of the home we'd shared for fourteen years, packing me (and two of the cats — Rhona kept Tilly the dog and Maxwell, her favourite ginger cat) off to my aunt Joan's house back in Earl Shilton. Who could blame her? I had grievously betrayed the love and trust she thought we shared for so many years. Which we did; but I lost my head for a space. *Mea culpa, mea culpa, mea maxima culpa.*

For several weeks I trailed disconsolately back and forth between Earl Shilton and Blaby to empty the latter property of my belongings; my clothes, my books, my CDs. Inevitably it was the lowest point in our entire relationship; in fact for a short time it looked as though after seventeen happy years the relationship was finally over and done with, finito Benito. I remained in Earl Shilton for four thoroughly bleak and miserable months over the cold, occasionally snowy winter of 2014-15. Rhona, now considering herself to be single, did her best to take care of the house, the dog and one of the other cats on her own. In Earl

Shilton Christmas 2014 came and went, dismally, greyly, emptily. Joan gamely did her best — I particularly appreciated the large bottle of Jack Daniels that she bought me; that didn't last long — but there was simply no comparison to the warmth and good cheer, the groaning table, the innumerable lights, the umpteen candles, the huge tree, the tinsel and baubles of so many prior Christmases in the grotto at Wareham Road.

I had no clue what the future might hold. I don't remember even thinking about it; trying to scrape through from one day to the next was about as much as I could do. I walked around the village daily; in the evenings I wrote in my diary at great length; I drank heavily (which significantly worsened the symptoms of my anxiety). All in all it was a thoroughly horrible, miserable period and in every respect I was at a very low ebb. But time passed, Christmas came and went, the new year of 2015 came and winter eased into spring; and with the regeneration of the natural world came a remarkable thing — a thaw not only of winter's ice and snow but a corresponding thaw of Rhona's anger toward me. By degrees we tentatively began to establish or rather re-establish a relationship of a kind. Rhona started to join my dad and Joan and me for lunches out and then, in time, meals out for just the two of us. She allowed me to take her to local eateries for a lunch or dinner on me and, on occasion, to get her a takeaway which we would eat at Joan's house. She allowed me to accompany her to hospital appointments and on shopping trips, to do house and garden jobs and chores back at Wareham Road that she couldn't do. Little by little Rhona relented. I don't know, will never now know and can't say, whether she was already feeling the first intimations of the illness which — unknown to us both — was about to overtake her or whether it was just the side-effect of four months away from and not being able to do without each other; but the establishment of a *détente* eventually became an obvious fact. "To be fully seen by somebody, then," writes Elizabeth Gilbert in *Committed*, "and be loved anyhow — this is a human offering that can border on the miraculous."

It's another fact that it took illness to bring us back together once and for all … or at least, once and for all until the end. I was sitting on my aunt's couch one afternoon — eight minutes past four o'clock, Friday

March 6th 2015 — when I received a text message from Rhona. *I'm not well.* Rather than get into another of our rounds of text tennis I rang her immediately. A weak and tired-sounding Rhona had suddenly come down with another bout of pyelonephritis — a kidney infection — and had taken to her bed. *Shall I come over to look after you and take care of the house?* I asked. She said that she was going to try to have a sleep first and we agreed to leave it for a couple of hours after which, rather than disturb her if she'd been asleep, I would wait to hear from her. But after only an hour or so Rhona rang again: *please come over.* I was only eight or so miles away and not doing anything so I was ideally fitted to drop everything, pack a bag with a few things and get a taxi over to Blaby immediately. I didn't know how long I would be staying — I might have remained just long enough until Rhona was better — but in actual fact I was walking back into my former home and to a large extent my old life with Rhona. Didn't see that coming, but that goes for plenty more besides, including how we got together in the first place so many years earlier.

These episodes of kidney infection were not in any sense new. On one otherwise normal evening in early 2010 Rhona had very suddenly come down with a bout of illness, characterised by frighteningly violent shivering (so violent that I could feel our inordinately heavy and sturdy bed shaking and rocking) and resulting in a late-night trip to Leicester Royal Infirmary, which turned out to be diagnosed as a bout of pyelonephritis — in short a kidney infection. This is a highly unpleasant but usually temporary condition, potentially serious but often (not always) easily treated by a course of antibiotics. This would recur occasionally at random intervals over the next few years, putting Rhona into bed or on the couch for a few days until it passed and her normally robust health resumed.

I arrived back at Wareham Road to find Rhona sleeping soundly upstairs in our bed. She had obviously decamped in a hurry; the fire and the television were both left on and a half-eaten plate of salad had been abandoned on the coffee table. I cleared up, turned off the telly and the fire and washed up. Later on a poorly but noticeably improved Rhona tottered downstairs. Following the familiar if irregular pattern, after a few days she recovered fully and was back on her feet again. That could well have been the signal for me to take myself back to Earl Shilton but it wasn't, because for the most part we picked up where we had left off four months earlier. By the spring of 2015 I was back at Wareham Road and life had resumed almost as it had been before the catastrophe of the previous year. True, I now had a separate bed in a separate bedroom and Rhona and I spent most (though by no means all) nights sleeping apart, but other than that change we resumed a life together and in so many ways it was as though we had never spent four months in different households. Life went back to its usual pattern. The cats had to be fed; the dog had to be walked; the lawn had to be mown; the washing washed and the ironing ironed; shopping bought and the daily household chores done. Life for Team Wowo in Wareham Road continued in its mundane sublunary way. I was back in my beloved surroundings but more than anything else I was back with my infinitely more beloved Rhona. We would soon be back in our lover's story, a line that Rhona would quote from time to time from David Bowie's song 'Kooks' (from 1971's *Hunky Dory*; technically a song about the love of a father for his baby son — Bowie's son Duncan — but one whose lyrics Rhona used to quote for that line about a lover's story). The thoroughly grim separation of almost four months — the longest time we ever spent apart in nearly twenty-one years — was at an end.

I had no inkling that life was about to put a bomb under both of our lives. Nobody does, or it wouldn't be a bomb. Sometimes life changes so slowly that any such change is at the time imperceptible and only viewable in hindsight; but at other times life can change — change radically, drastically at that — in the blink of an eye, with a single dramatic event, with the metaphorical turn of a card or the toss of a coin or a throw of the dice. It had done so in November 2014; on Tuesday July 21st 2015 it would do so again.

Chapter Nine

The Toss of a Coin

God made the world round so we would never
be able to see too far down the road.
—Isak Dinesen (Karen Blixen)

In early July of 2015 Rhona and her mum went on a Mediterranean cruise; she agreed to leave me behind at Wareham Road to take care of the house and the pets in her absence. She visited Turkey, Cyprus and — for Rhona the most exciting of all, which she would often refer to later on — Israel; a very brief stop-over at Tel Aviv which she found marvellous. She had achieved a long-standing ambition and had finally made it, even if only for a few hours, to Israeli soil.

Just a few days back from her sun-kissed holiday, on the morning of Tuesday July 21st 2015 a tanned and relaxed Rhona got out of bed and suddenly found that she could barely hobble let alone walk; both of her legs were incredibly painful. From the waist down she had gone from a plump but healthy sixty-four year-old to a superannuated cripple. This seemed ominous because four years earlier in 2011 she had had a deep vein thrombosis in the popliteal vein in the back of one leg immediately after a long flight from the USA, necessitating months of treatment with warfarin. Fast forward four years and Rhona of course had just had another flight — not as lengthy but still significant — back from Turkey. It didn't look good.

We made it somehow to the local surgery where a GP took a look at Rhona's legs. While not offering a definitive diagnosis he too suspected a flight-induced DVT and packed us off, more or less immediately given the potential seriousness of the condition, to Leicester Royal Infirmary for further testing. I don't recall too much about that day (by the end of it I was too busy and too tired to have written it up in my diary as I would normally have done) but I do recall being there until well on into the evening until the department we were in closed down and being asked to go home and come back the following day. We did so; and by the end of that second day it had been determined, after much testing, that Rhona's kidneys had failed almost completely. This time there was no kidney infection; she was now in full-blown end-stage renal failure and was admitted to the Infirmary immediately.

We were now decisively and decidedly in the Kingdom of the Chronically Sick. Whether it comes incrementally and by degrees or descends from nowhere out of a clear blue sky, being handed down such a diagnosis means that life has changed massively and irrevocably and will never again be what it has been before. It means that life becomes a round of hospital appointments, tests, procedures, medication; long waits in dreary corridors looking at posters on the wall, conversations with sundry medical experts, pharmacies, prescriptions. It entails learning a wholly new vocabulary — Hickman line; permacath; eGFR; Allevyn gentle border — and a litany of drugs: Renacet; Forceval; Fostair; Alfacalcidol; urokinase; alteplase; warfarin. Leicester has three main NHS hospitals — the Leicester Royal Infirmary; Leicester General; and Glenfield — and over the next three-and-a-bit years we would have innumerable appointments in each, spend uncountable hours in each and come to know them all far, far more intimately than anybody ever should who doesn't work there.

Kidney failure. With the benefit of always perfect hindsight we might have seen this or something like it coming. Rhona had had certain kidney problems for several years previously, as already detailed, beginning with her first bout of pyelonephritis in 2010. The following year it was determined that Rhona had a stone in one of her kidneys which was successfully removed but required the implantation of a stent for several weeks which she found profoundly debilitating and extremely miserable until it was removed. After that she felt well and had several years of normal health with only intermittent recurrences of the pyelonephritis, occasional flare-ups; but now all of that was up-ended. Now she didn't have kidney stones or now-and-again bouts of kidney infection but was in pretty well complete kidney failure.

Looking back on it all now from the viewpoint of several years, in retrospect it's pretty clear to see that the kidney stone and the repeated bouts of kidney infection had done serious, in fact irreparable damage to both of her kidneys, but of course at the time we didn't know this. Neither of us could have imagined that these episodes were to result in such profound harm to her kidneys that she would succumb to end-stage renal failure. The kidney stone had been removed and, although disagreeable for a few days, the bouts of kidney infection were manageable and managed and in any case few and far between. Neither of us could have foreseen that these things combined would result in what was to happen next.

Sitting by her side, in an ambulance Rhona was transferred very late one night from Leicester Royal Infirmary to the Leicester General hospital across the city, where she would spend the next several weeks. Not a driver, over those weeks I spent hundreds of pounds (I once totted it up roughly to have cost more than seven hundred quid) on taxis on a nearly daily basis to get me to the General in order to see Rhona, to take in what she wanted and needed and to spend as much time with her at the bedside as visiting hours allowed. Almost every day I got a taxi from Blaby to the General, taking in the things that Rhona had asked for — clean nighties and knickers; certain foods and the like —, helping her to have a decent shower as she was still too weak and debilitated to do it by herself and spending as long with her as I was able before returning to an empty home and getting something resembling food cobbled together for supper before bedtime and then repeating the process the following day.

In end-stage renal failure there are only two options if you hope to keep the patient — or indeed yourself — alive; the short-term measure of haemodialysis, where some of the failed organs' function is taken over by a dialysis machine, or if you're looking for a (hopefully) permanent cure, a kidney transplant. At this early stage there was still some residual hope on the part of the medical team that Rhona's kidney function could be brought back up to the point — just — where haemodialysis wouldn't be needed. That hope seemed to be justified. The day came, many weeks after her initial admission, when it was determined that Rhona was well enough to be discharged. Safely ensconced back at home at Wareham Road she was unable to walk or even do much, if anything, for herself. For a considerable time she was in effect largely helpless and I became her full-time carer. I am the diametric opposite of a conservative and nobody's idea of a traditionalist in very much but I regret that Rhona and I never married. I would have done so but it was something that we never discussed, possibly because Rhona had had a slight feeling of being press-ganged into the marriage she'd had and because she saw no reason, no need to change the set-up that we already had. As I've said previously I am not a religious man but still, for all my adherence to Jew-ish-ness I took the traditional Anglican wedding vows very seriously even in the absence of a marriage licence: *for better, for worse, for richer, for poorer, in sickness and in health, to love and to cherish, till death us do part.* I'm not even a believer let alone a Christian but as far as relationships go these words matter to me. *In sickness and in health.* I made up a bed for Rhona on the couch in the living room and she would remain there for many weeks beneath a duvet (and usually beneath a cat), unable to hobble further than the downstairs lavatory and even then slowly, painfully, haltingly, limping with a walking frame lent by the hospital. Every morning I washed her all over, bed-bath style, with a bowl of hot water, soap and a flannel on the coffee table and changed her underwear and nightdress and then set about preparing the first meal of the day. For complex medical reasons I won't go into, certain normal components of food are a particular problem for renal patients — potassium and phosphates especially — and a special renal diet has to be followed; some foods are contraindicated outright (Rhona had to give up on her beloved tomatoes and grapefruit juice; potassium-rich bananas were also *verboten*) and vegetables need to have their nutrients, so essential to the healthy, leached out of them by lengthy soaking in several changes of water before cooking. Most large-scale shopping was done online and delivered to the house; a top-up of the basics could be carried out by me in the local shops reachable on foot. For a short space district nurses visited every week to teach me how to give Rhona injections of various medications — I think erythropoietin to stimulate the formation of red blood cells, and heparin which is an anticoagulant — directly into the skin of her belly. With an incredibly short, stubby needle this wasn't quite the ordeal that it may sound and in any case didn't last long.

For a time Rhona had a nephrostomy — an artificial opening between her kidney and the outside world, a slender plastic tube inserted into a small dressing-protected incision in her back which collected urine in a plastic bag of which there were two; a night bag and a day bag, both of which had to be emptied and disposed of. While this lasted the first job of the morning once I was up was to get rid of the night bag and attach the day bag. Detach night bag; empty down the lavatory; throw away; reattach new bag. So it goes; that's how it works. On one night a few weeks into this new phase Rhona, presumably through turning over perhaps more roughly than usual on the couch-bed, managed to dislodge the tube and was taken by ambulance back into hospital. Whether it had been working as it should or not I don't now remember but soon afterwards the nephrostomy was removed and there was no more daily emptying and changing of bags.

For those first few months of kidney failure Rhona was in and out of the General, dividing her days between home and hospital; at home when deemed well enough to be there, back in hospital when something went wrong or for a particular medical procedure or simply as the medicos tried to rekindle some semblance of kidney function. It shouldn't be the case but many of my memories of Rhona at this time are of her in one of her umpteen nighties propped up in a hospital bed on a urology ward in the General. At around this time adult colouring books enjoyed a brief vogue and Rhona spent many a bed-bound but by all appearances relatively comfortable hour with her colouring books and felt-tipped pens. I brought in Thermos flasks of ice for her drinks. Nearby friends brought in Chinese takeaways, burgers and fries from well-known fast-food outlets to augment the hospital food; for all the seriousness of her condition, even now her appetite was undiminished.

That was when she was an in-patient. When at home, on a day-to-day basis in these first few weeks and months of renal failure just about everything was carried out by me. Ironically it wasn't until well after Rhona's death that I discovered how many organisations are out there to offer practical and emotional support to those caring for someone who is chronically ill; at the time I had no idea and in any case even in the most trying circumstances it never entered my head to seek outside assistance. Looking after Rhona was my job and I took a proprietorial, even a jealous sense of pride in it. I had come back to Blaby in order to care for Rhona (and this was even when she was experiencing another short-term bout of pyelonephritis rather than full-blown kidney failure); caring for Rhona was exactly what I was going to do. Other people feel differently, however. In the UK as of 2019 there are around six and a half million carers — that's almost one in seven people — of whom about 42% are men. Three in five people can expect to be a carer at some point in their lives, a figure projected to rise by around two million per year; that's six thousand every day. It's estimated that the economic contribution made by this silent army of carers is over £130 billion annually. Carers occupy all age groups — very young or even child carers are a particularly pressing issue — but one in five people aged between fifty and sixty-four are carers; in the sixty to ninety-four age bracket 65% of carers have a long-term health problem or disability themselves. The stress and strain of caring for someone who is chronically ill — sometimes juggling work at the same time and frequently facing serious financial pressures — means that the health burden is huge. Carers are themselves twice as likely to be sick and/or disabled; one survey found that 72% said that they'd experienced mental health problems and 62% physical ill health as a result of caring. Those providing a high level of care are at a 23% greater risk of suffering a stroke. Having been there, done that and worn the latex gloves myself I now see this as one of the great crisis issues of our time, though one that in my opinion is criminally unknown to the general public and woefully under-reported.

Be that as it may: all of this amounted to an even more insular, cloistered and isolated existence than before which — obviously apart from its cause — suited me just fine. Rhona and I had each other to ourselves even more than had ever before been the case; Rhona on her couch-bed watching her favourite things on the telly, me busying myself with her care and with looking after our home, the garden, the dog, the cats, the shopping, the cooking. Even so, lest I paint a wholly false picture of the noble carer tenderly mopping the fevered brow of the stoic and uncomplaining-bordering-on-saintly patient, there were some fraught moments, usually when I was feeling frazzled and run ragged by the demands of tending to Rhona and the attitude of ingratitude that she (only rarely, in all fairness) demonstrated that nothing I did was right. In *All At Sea* Decca Aitkenhead writes sagely of the tendency to deify our dead loved ones; to gloss over the faults, to soft-pedal the irritating habits, to cast the petty annoyances and frank rows in romantic soft focus. It's a dangerous delusion, however natural and understandable it may be. Like all couples we had our disagreements from time to time; I wouldn't believe any couple who said that they didn't (and more to the point I wouldn't trust them; if true it suggests an anaemic lack of spirit only considered admirable in sheep). Of course we did; from minor, trivial niggles to (admittedly extremely rare) blazing rows. In *The Widower's Notebook* Jonathan Santlofer recalls:

> I remember helping my mother clean out my father's closets after he died, listening to her idealize him until I'd finally had enough. "In case you forgot," I said, in a teasing tone, "he was also a pain in the ass." My mother didn't miss a beat: "But he was *my* pain in the ass."

So often worn down by the burden of chronic illness with all that that entails and caring respectively, we sometimes — again, very seldom — had a spat. I recall one particular occasion when a meal (I don't remember what it was) over which I thought I'd spent an inordinate amount of care and lavished a great deal of love, brought in proudly from the kitchen and placed on Rhona's lap tray, apparently had something or other wrong with just about every item of it. Bewildered, disappointed and irate I responded by furiously launching my laptop against the wall of the dining room not just once but twice, smashing it to splintered plastic smithereens far beyond any hope of repair. I considered this preferable to launching it at Rhona, which was my initial impulse. Such moments, though perhaps almost inevitable given the situation we found ourselves in, were mercifully exceptionally rare. Yes, infrequently she could be a pain in the arse whether in sickness or in health, but then goodness knows so could I and then some. I gave Rhona far, far, *far* more to have to put up with than vice versa. And in any case, even if she was very rarely a pain in the arse, she was *my* pain in the arse. Overwhelmingly, harmony reigned supreme. As I've previously mentioned, a friend of ours who claimed to be able to pick up on such things visited us once and remarked what a calm, peaceful and harmonious atmosphere prevailed in our home.

As already noted, for a lengthy period Rhona was unable to walk, but thanks to the General she was supplied with a walking frame and thanks to the British Red Cross we were given the indefinite use of a wheelchair, and in due course I was able to take her out in our neighbourhood on fine days for a slow trundle around the local streets to enjoy the cool and cooling but beautiful autumnal afternoon sunshine. Eventually she was able to drive again (I have never deeply regretted not learning to drive and have never missed it, but there have been moments …) and I also pushed her around local supermarkets, basket on lap, and to the hairdresser to make her feel pampered. Eventually she was able to haul herself up the stairs and to have a shower unaided (although she was still sufficiently frail for a while longer to have to do so sitting down, so I bought her a shower stool). It was the slow beginning of a return to something almost, but not quite, like a normal life.

Except that it was inevitably a new and different kind of normal. Things didn't change significantly until October 2015 when, back at the General and with me at her side holding her hand (though studiously looking elsewhere), Rhona had a permacath or Hickman line inserted into the jugular vein on the right side of her neck — a thin plastic tube threaded down around her heart with two dangling valves sitting just above or even in her bra that allowed her to receive dialysis — and she began haemodialysis three times a week at a dedicated renal unit in Hamilton on the other side of Leicester. Initially she started on the early shift but eventually moved to the later one, being collected at 4:00pm by a car specially laid on for renal patients in the area. It's possible — albeit tricky — to dialyse at home and this is something that at one point we looked into, even to the extent of being visited by a nurse who came out to size up the spare room where it would have been done. I was certainly more than prepared to undergo the necessary training to teach me how to attach Rhona to and detach her from a dialysis machine and to keep everything running in good order. However, home dialysis does involve considerable upheaval to the fabric of one's house — dialysis relies on a constant supply of water and to have dialysed at home would have meant a great deal of plumbing to run water from the bathroom to the spare bedroom — but moreover I think Rhona found it better to keep dialysis out of, away from our home; to keep it psychologically or emotionally at arm's length (at least as far as such a thing was possible) by dialysing at the renal unit. I don't believe there was anything like denial in this; I do think it was Rhona's way of keeping her home life and renal failure life fairly sharply demarcated. Dialysis at Hamilton was unavoidable but home was home and was sacrosanct.

It was haemodialysis that made Rhona turn the corner in terms of her health as she made a slow but steady improvement thereafter. Eventually the walking frame and shower stool were banished to the garage, our permanent dumping ground which we used to clear out every year only for it to fill up again. Eventually the wheelchair was returned to the British Red Cross. Dialysis is a long way from perfect and nobody would claim otherwise but it takes over *some* of the functioning of failed kidneys — albeit little; around 10% of a healthy, normally functioning organ — and now Rhona began to improve, in time regaining a fair degree of her lost strength and mobility. Dialysis is a major commitment however and many renal patients find it a serious inconvenience; some actively refuse it and allow renal failure to end their lives, which usually comes about in short order. Although transport was provided — she was collected from and dropped off back at home — the specialist dialysis unit was on the other side of Leicester; with other dialysis patients to collect and drop off the journey there and back could take close to an hour each time. And a dialysis session itself lasts for four hours; four hours connected to a slowly spinning machine doing a small part of the job of failed kidneys in extracting toxins from the bloodstream. For Rhona this was a combined time of some six to seven hours away from home three times a week — Tuesday, Thursday and Saturday without fail, no exceptions; she would return home somewhere between 10:30 and 11:00pm and struggle straight up to bed feeling wretched. Nevertheless it was keeping her alive. It became a routine, as I say our new normal to which we both — but Rhona especially of course — had to adapt.

All the same the hard truth is that it's a myth that patients with end-stage kidney failure can survive indefinitely on dialysis. In fact research has shown that the average survival rate for dialysis patients is around five to ten years (though this is only the average; inevitably there are cases where some patients survive on dialysis for far longer. I recently heard of the case of a woman who had been on dialysis for fifteen years, though this is very much an exception). Dialysis can and does keep renal failure patients alive but not for ever; it's never anything other than a stopgap, a temporary measure. The only hope of a permanent cure and the only chance of a relatively normal dialysis-free life is kidney transplantation. Survival rates whether from living or deceased donors are extremely good and have little difference between them. Rhona was on the waiting list; we were told that the phone call from the hospital to inform us that an organ has become available — from whatever source, living or dead — can come at literally any moment, even to the extent of being instructed to keep a bag packed and to be ready to drop everything and head off to the hospital there and then.

With all these things in mind, after Rhona had had several months on dialysis I decided after very little thought — I say very little but in actuality none was necessary — that I would offer myself as a living donor and try to give Rhona one of my own kidneys. This is a lengthy, involved process and a serious business. The surgery is comparatively easier on the donor than the recipient — without complications a donor can be out of hospital within a few days and fully recovered within a few weeks; for the recipient it's often a somewhat steeper challenge — but it is a major operation all the same. It's perfectly possible to live a normal, healthy and active life with just one kidney (indeed, I discovered that some people are naturally born with a single kidney, a fact which can sometimes be picked up only in the course of examination for something else entirely). With the human body's remarkable recuperative powers the remaining organ takes up some of the function of the donated one. Post-donation life requires a few lifestyle adjustments (watch the weight; cut out the salt; keep an eye on the blood pressure, which can tend to rise over time unless carefully and periodically monitored; stay off the booze and so forth — only the last gave me the very briefest of pauses) but generally speaking those living donors who sacrifice a kidney can expect to live as long and as healthily as anybody else since only those who are healthy enough to begin with are considered suitable to donate. It didn't require rumination. *I have two kidneys and I only need the one. Rhona needs one. Here, take one of mine.*

The emotional component for the prospective donor is given as much weight as the physical; anybody electing to donate an organ is given a thorough psychological evaluation to determine their motives for doing so (that's to say, that there's no element of compulsion or coercion), how they are likely to cope in the aftermath of serious surgery with all that that entails and how they might react should the transplantation be unsuccessful, which unfortunately is sometimes the case. While I can understand the need for a certain amount of this in my opinion and experience far too much was made of it. Time and time again, as Rhona and I sat in a dingy little office as yet another kind of medico spelt out the potential risks, I silently said to myself: *Oh, for fuck's sake; we haven't got much time here. I'm* volunteering *for this and don't* care *about the risks. I'm doing this because I want to. Just fucking get* on *with it, will you?*

The transplant coordinator at Leicester's General hospital set the wheels of the testing process in motion. I was given huge amounts of literature to read containing everything you never wanted to know about kidney failure and kidney transplantation and plenty more besides. Rhona and I attended lectures by transplant surgeons to prospective donors and recipients. The lecture theatre was full of the sick and those who wanted to make them better; parents and children, brothers and sisters, spouses, partners, friends. There were consultations aplenty to the point of weariness; the transplant coordinator, this surgeon, that consultant, this doctor, that nurse. Finally the physical testing started. Physical examinations; multiple blood tests — prospective donation is not something for anyone afraid of needles, although the sheer amount of times that you're punctured may cure you of that particular fear I suppose —, X-rays and finally an eGFR test (estimated glomerular filtration rate. I think I'll stick to eGFR) which consists of an injection of a small amount of radioactive tracer and blood tests at hourly intervals for the following five hours to determine how well — or not — the kidneys excrete the substance. I admit to a superstitious fear of radioactivity and wasn't wildly enthused about the idea of having some radioactive liquid injected into my bloodstream but I was reassured that the amount of said substance (technetium, I think) is minuscule and that the procedure is safe and so on June 21st 2016 — a bright, sunny and warm midsummer day — I went to Leicester Royal Infirmary's Department of Nuclear Medicine and underwent the eGFR test. Following the injection Rhona and I took ourselves off to the Infirmary's café for a drink and a snack for a couple of hours until I returned to the department for the first of several blood tests, thereafter one an hour for several hours until it was time to go home. Afterwards I was very mildly radioactive for several weeks and was told to flush the toilet twice after going and to wash my hands more thoroughly and scrupulously than usual. If I was planning to go abroad within the next three months (not that I was) my slight radioactivity would show up on airport scanning equipment so the Infirmary could provide me with a letter to say that I wasn't an international terrorist mastermind trying to smuggle stolen nuclear material for a dirty bomb but that this was a result of a medical procedure.

By sheer coincidence it turned out that Rhona and I had the same comparatively uncommon blood group, O negative, which according to the NHS is shared by only 13% of the population (compared to 35% for O positive for example which is the most common blood group). Transplantation across blood groups is at least some of the time possible but cross-blood transplantation requires an onslaught of extra medication for the rest of the recipient's life to overcome the problem of rejection over and above the life-long cocktail of drugs that evenly-matched recipients have to take. The fact that Rhona and I almost miraculously had the same relatively rare blood group was a major hurdle cleared. It looked as though I was in the frame to be able to sacrifice one of my own kidneys to give Rhona a shot at returning to a normal life, and anxiously we waited for the results of my eGFR test. In the meantime, carrying a few more pounds than I should have been, I was instructed to lose some weight and so I gave up the booze and went on a crash diet.

For obvious reasons dialysis three times a week for hours at a time places some severe constraints on one's ability to travel but with sufficient planning it is possible to dialyse away from home at another hospital or renal unit. (There are even special holidays, including cruises, for renal patients where dialysis is provided). Rhona had made arrangements to visit her mother and brother in Newcastle for a week and to dialyse at the city's Freeman hospital. By sheer bad luck it was on one of those days while she was away that, at the end of June, not long after the eGFR, just after I'd got up I received a phone call from the transplant coordinator at the General.

It was bad news.

I'm very sorry. Your kidney function isn't quite good enough to be able to donate, she said, or words to that effect. I don't understand the units of measurement used but the minimum value for donation and a healthy life thereafter is 80; my kidney function stood at 70. Ironically and almost unbelievably the tests had revealed that, though very much milder than Rhona's end-stage renal failure, I too had — have — a slight degree of kidney impairment, not serious enough to warrant treatment but enough to knock me out of the running to donate one kidney and live on the function of the other. *OK*, I said, *but even so, can't you …?* No, they can't. *Is there anything I can do to improve it?* No, there isn't. It was no go. I was out of the race. Medical confidentiality or data protection or whatever other bullshit is involved these days meant that the coordinator wasn't even allowed to tell Rhona; I had to call her in Newcastle and break the bad news myself. *Look, Rhona … I think you should prepare yourself … I've just had a phone call …*

Chapter Ten

Heartbreak

Hearts can break. Yes, hearts can break. Sometimes I think it would be better if we died when they did, but we don't.
—Stephen King: *Hearts in Atlantis*

Since I'd been knocked out of the running to be a living donor Rhona remained on the transplant list awaiting a donated kidney. Despite her illness and thrice-weekly dialysis, life continued in its usual measured course, as per usual changing little and slowly at Wareham Road. As an events organiser Rhona continued to plan and stage beauty pageants each year; every winter we organised the distribution of the Yellow Pages in the area; she went from being a desultory to a dedicated-going-on-fanatical eBayer, buying up stock from local charity shops and factory outlets and listing from her cherished iPad, parcels being sent practically every other day from the nearby post office. Apart from the issue of Rhona's condition we had a quiet, even a small but a wonderful life together; unspectacular, certainly, unshowy, humble and without overt excitement but with steadiness, reliability, even predictability and with joy in its own way and with never anything other than love. After the brief break of 2014-15 the *modus vivendi* held strong.

Time passed. By the summer of 2018 I had through my own efforts lost over four stones in weight (that's close to 30kg for those who work in new money) and I wondered if this weight loss might make a difference to kidney donation. I recalled that my previous attempt at kidney donation had involved losing weight so now, very substantially lighter, I thought that I could have a second chance at donating a kidney. The transplant coordinator must have thought so too since when I contacted her with this snippet of news she agreed that I could go through the testing process for kidney donation a second time in a little over two years. I submitted to the same testing procedures that I had gone through two years earlier; all the same physical examinations, all the same blood tests, all the same X-rays, a second eGFR on August 21st 2018.

And yet it was still not to be. The fairly drastic weight loss had made not a jot of difference; in June 2016 my kidney function had been 70 (of whatever measurement it is) and now in August 2018 it was barely changed at 69. I was, once and for all, ruled out as a potential living donor. I had — *Rhona* had — been offered a second bite at the cherry but now there would be no third chance, no third attempt at testing. There would simply be no point. If Rhona was going to receive a donated kidney to give her a normal life back it wouldn't be coming from me.

As if that wasn't bad enough, even worse was to come.

We had learnt that many renal patients succumb not to the failure of their kidneys but to heart-related conditions. Most dialysis patients ultimately die of cardiovascular disease; heart-related mortality is 10-20 times higher in renal patients than in the general population. As well as end-stage renal failure, to add to Wo's woes in about the last year of her life Rhona developed heart failure — specifically a condition called aortic stenosis in which the aortic valve becomes narrowed and constricted, making the heart have to work harder to pump blood, leading to fatigue, debility, breathlessness, swollen legs and a host of other symptoms. It's a progressive condition and one of the most serious cardiovascular illnesses; after diagnosis people with severe AS have survival rates of 50% at two years and only 20% at five years without valve replacement surgery, which, although major cardiac surgery in anybody's book, is the only thing that potentially offers a complete cure. Quite apart from anything kidney-related, visits to various hospitals continued to pile up; across 2018 Rhona underwent a battery of diagnostic tests — an echocardiogram, an ECG and an angiogram among them — to determine the severity of the condition. The results of the angiogram meant that she was due ultimately for valve replacement surgery but the appointment came too late for her. She would of course still have had kidney failure, but one of the many unanswerable, tormenting questions is whether Rhona would still be here with me now and still on dialysis if that valve replacement surgery had been performed in time. It's one of the many things that I'll never know.

As 2015 became 2016 gradually Rhona had gone from being a couch-bound and more or less helpless invalid unable to limp any further than the downstairs lavatory to someone virtually fully mobile — slower than before, undoubtedly, but still mobile. After the initial failure of her kidneys haemodialysis had given Rhona at least something of her life back; now in 2018 heart failure began slowly to claw it away from her again. Chronic serious illness shrinks life to a regular and wearying round of hospital appointments, tests and procedures; daily pills by the handful — vitamin supplements; phosphate binders; calcium supplements; anticoagulants. Now with heart failure as well as kidney failure Rhona's life shrank further still; visits to the local surgery and to all three of Leicester's main hospitals increased. Her appetite had been waning for a while and over time she lost a great deal of weight. The — let's be honest here — fairly hefty woman of yore was slowly disappearing. She must have been one of the few patients ever recommended by any medical professional to eat fattening, calorie-laden foods. ("Plenty of cream cakes" she was advised by her nephrologist). But she found gustatory enjoyment in sandwiches (especially ham and pease pudding, a legacy of her upbringing in the north-east), cheese on toast, the occasional takeaway, chip-shop chips (typical order: chips, battered sausage, small curry sauce and occasionally the, to me, frankly repulsive pineapple fritter) and — especially — in eating out which we had always loved and had done regularly but now, along with selling on eBay, became her last great pleasure in the years of her illness and even more so in what would prove to be the final months of her life. At the local Chinese restaurant or a nearby steakhouse we could be assured that, for the most part unlike at home, she would eat a hearty meal and do it full justice, so toward the end we were eating out a couple of times a week on my coin. These were some of the very happiest experiences in what could so easily have otherwise been a gloomy, even bleak time, as so many photographs taken on my smartphone can attest. In that last year the image of Rhona beaming over a rare fillet steak with all the trimmings — far and away her favourite meal as a dedicated carnist — is amongst the happiest memories I have of her.

Rhona grew slowly but progressively thinner, weaker, less able. Out and about we had always held hands or linked arms; now she clung to me much more and more tightly just to get around as her strength diminished and breathing became more effortful. At home the stairs were easily her greatest challenge, her domestic version of Mount Everest. Because this was the case she tended, in this final year, to spend as much time as possible either upstairs or downstairs to obviate the need to climb the thirteen steps to the upper floor any more than she needed to. A devoted (in fact bordering on fanatical) eBayer, Rhona was able to carry on with her hobby-cum-business from a sitting position with her beloved and much-used iPad, lying either on the bed upstairs or the couch downstairs. I don't claim to be any kind of expert in any way whatsoever but I'm a reasonably good cook; as I've said previously at the age of twenty, during a period of unemployment, I got into cooking in quite a big way for a time and never quite lost the bug. As I've also said Rhona's appetite ebbed and I spent a great deal of time suggesting tasty treats which she might enjoy that I could prepare for her; for the most part the big woman who a few years before could and regularly did eat a colossal meal and somehow still leave room for an equally generous pudding and was like me a dedicated viewer of certain cookery programmes on TV now wanted small, light meals, especially sandwiches but, on occasion, something more substantial such as Jamie Oliver's steak (rare, of course) with flash-fried liver and onion gravy, carefully prepared by this long-time vegetarian-going-on-vegan. Having spent a good deal of time slicing and cooking cold and slimy liver and doing my best to cook a rare steak, "You must love me" she declared once, smiling, as she cleared her plate on the lap tray before her. With younger and healthier legs I mounted the stairs ten or a dozen times a day to Rhona in her nightie or bathrobe, propped up on the bed, iPad in hand, bearing a lap tray with a sandwich (explicit instructions given and followed to the letter … usually) and tea in her favourite white bullet mug. Up, down, up, down, up, down, up, down. It was tiring, certainly; it was also a true privilege.

Rhona and I, staunch old-time socialists both (we joined the Labour party when Jeremy Corbyn was elected leader), were ardent, passionate supporters of the NHS — I still am — but nothing happens quickly and, as I now know with the benefit of always perfect hindsight, time was running out. It was, it is, our tragedy that we were not to know just how quickly it was running out. One appointment for an angiogram, Rhona prepared and in a hospital gown, bed and all, was cancelled after a long and wasted day on the ward due to the volume of emergency cases on that particular day. A second appointment a few weeks later — hospital gown, bed once more — was cancelled because Rhona's INR (she was again being treated with warfarin) was too high, making any kind of invasive procedure unsafe due to the risk of uncontrollable bleeding. She did finally have the angiogram toward the end of September and the way was then clear for valve replacement surgery; dying as suddenly as she did she simply ran out of time. I think it would be fair to say that Rhona died *with* kidney disease but *of* heart disease, as is usually the case with renal patients. Had those first two appointments not been cancelled and had the angiogram taken place when initially scheduled — therefore valve replacement surgery taking place earlier — would Rhona still be here, albeit still on dialysis? Another regularly asked but ultimately unanswerable question, of which there are all too many.

Following a fall in the first week of 2018 my dad, then eighty-five, broke his hip, developed pneumonia ('the old man's friend') and after several weeks in Nuneaton's George Eliot hospital died in February. At the age of forty-six I was an orphan. Rhona had taken both me and my aunt Joan to the hospital regularly in those final weeks of his life though Rhona herself — compromised by her illnesses and prey to opportunistic infections — was unable to see him apart from through the glass in the door of his tiny room. Even Joan and I were scarily gowned, masked and gloved. Entirely unlike with my mum, my dad and I had not had an especially close relationship (it had been civil rather than warm) and although this doesn't make me look good, if I'm honest I felt no great grief at his passing. All the same Rhona, as poorly as she was, was with me throughout, from the first day in hospital all the way through to the funeral on a grey, wind-lashed, rain-soaked March day.

Isak Dinesen (Karen Blixen) wrote that God made the world round so that we wouldn't be able to see too far down the road. I've learnt the hard way to appreciate the tragic wisdom in that observation. Hindsight is always perfect; I of course know now but didn't know then, had no reason to suspect, that 2018 with its sweltering summer heatwave would turn out to be the last year of Rhona's life. Previously in this account I have said that life can change drastically — for the better or for the worse — on the spin of a coin, at random, unforeseen and unexpected events that strike out of the blue. For me it did so in December 1997. It did so in November 2014. It did so again in July 2015. Now it was to do so — irreparably; unmendably — in November 2018.

Chapter Eleven

Three Days in November

> When you look at a chair, it has a clear purpose: to be sat on. A spoon is for eating soup. Much of the time, when I consider what happens to us, it seems that the purpose of life is to suffer in agony and die.
>
> —William Trout: *Last Notebooks*

As 2018 approached its end Rhona had endured haemodialysis three days a week every week without fail for a little over three years. Although a heavy burden on her physically and in terms of swallowing up so much of her time it had, paradoxically perhaps, become a regular, predictable routine; picked up at 4:00pm every Tuesday, Thursday and Saturday, blanket, iPhone, iPad, sandwiches, Wotsits and Edwardian mints in her dialysis bag, back at around 10:30pm, struggling slowly up the stairs straight to bed and asleep within minutes with LBC playing quietly through the night on the TV. To a greater or a lesser extent there was always something of a small cloud over dialysis days; the knowledge that the sandwiches would have to be made, the bag prepared and that the transport would arrive at four o'clock to whisk her away for another six or seven hours before coming back home for a weary, arduous trudge up the stairs to bed. All the same, until the phone call for a transplant came through it was her lifeline and in the final three years that routine became our life together.

Not that it was without its problems. Very far from it. Despite the name a permacath (alias Hickman line) isn't intended to be permanent and is only supposed to be a temporary measure typically ahead of the creation of a fistula on the inside of the forearm, something that Rhona emphatically, vehemently did not want. A permacath of this nature has a tendency to form blood clots on the end of the tube inside the body closest to the heart and this happened to Rhona; her first permacath was replaced in 2017. Clotting is mildly dangerous but moreover makes for poor dialysis and creates a need to be treated with infusions of thrombolytic drugs such as urokinase and alteplase, the process being painless but taking several dragging hours back on a hospital bed. In what turned out to be the last year of her life the number of visits we made to the General for these infusions and the number of hours spent in so doing are almost beyond counting. At dialysis Rhona and I were constantly in touch by text message; at some point in the evening I would always send her the usual message reading *How's it going?* to which all too often she would respond negatively. Possibly fifty per cent of the time at least this would mean a trip to the General a day or two later for another infusion of the clot-busting wonder drugs which would rectify the situation for a few sessions — if we were lucky; we were not always — until the pattern repeated itself.

All the same this was what I've called the new normal and the pattern of our life together for those final three years; since the failure of her kidneys in July 2015 and the beginning of dialysis in October of that year the highly abnormal had become our life. Of necessity it had become a small life in a small world, I concede; small, certainly, but in its own way beautiful. Though easily tired (latterly due far more to the aortic stenosis, though of course kidney failure doesn't help much) she regained some mobility and we were able to get out and about to shop regularly — predominantly for food, for household items, for the bread and fillings for her beloved sandwiches, to charity shops for eBay stock to be listed later and sold at a profit, sent from a local post office which we visited almost every other day. Non-dialysis days

— Monday; Wednesday; Friday; Sunday — were referred to by Rhona as her days off, as though dialysis was a full-time occupation and every other day was a welcome, in fact blessed release and relief, which is wholly understandable. We tried to make the most of them. They were the good days. More than that; they were some of the very best days we ever knew. Distance lends enchantment to the view, it's said, but I kept a written and photographic record of our life together and in some cases hindsight can clarify as much as it can obscure. Though ill, Rhona hadn't been given a terminal diagnosis; though frail and easily exhausted, in the last year of her life she tried to maintain a routine of shopping, eBaying, eating out on a regular basis and other small pleasures. Both in Stevenage and Blaby we had enjoyed eating out often; in this final year we stepped it up considerably. With that hindsight again it's almost as though we knew the end was near. We didn't, of course, but looking back on it now it looks that way.

After my dad's death in February 2018 and the sale of his house in October of that year I'd come into some money for the first time in my life and I was determined to put it to the best possible use I knew: by treating Rhona on a grander scale than had hitherto obtained. We'd had no kind of holiday or even a short break worthy of the name since a few sunny days in Rutland in the summer of 2010; now, with a fairly substantial cushion of cash, I wanted to take a giant leap up from a good meal in a good restaurant or a book or a DVD and was keen to take Rhona away and give her a bit of the high life, a taste of as much luxury as money can buy. Ill as she was and with her life dominated by thrice-weekly dialysis and umpteen hospital appointments planned and unplanned, I thought that she needed to be treated to a taste of gracious living. Nobody deserved it more. Of necessity it couldn't be for longer than three days, dodging dialysis sessions between Saturday and Tuesday. Online I researched luxury boutique hotels and threw a lengthy list of them at Rhona; she chose — partly on the basis of liking the name, she said, but also because it had a lift — Dumbleton Hall not far from Evesham, a vast, sprawling country manor of umpteen rooms set in nineteen acres of grounds just inside the border of Gloucestershire, built of creamy Cotswold stone on the site of its ancient predecessor and completed in 1832. Though there for only two-and-a-bit days in mid-October we had the most fantastic time imaginable, sleeping soundly in a sumptuous four-poster bed in the grand, high-ceilinged Malvern suite, eating delicious breakfasts and dinners in the restaurant, hobnobbing with the (often retired) well-heeled and evidently wealthy fellow guests. Not even a cold, windy, rainy day spent haunting the charity shops of the lovely town of Evesham — for which Rhona hired and loved using a mobility scooter for a few hours to get around — could dampen what was a thoroughly wonderful experience. Brief it may have had to have been but it was one of the most beautiful of so many beautiful experiences that we shared whether in sickness or in health. Not for the first time by any means but for the first time in a long time we had had a little taste of the high life and came home thinking, *oh yes, we're doing more of this.*

As it turned out, it came just in the nick of time. We didn't do more of that because we didn't get the chance.

Toward the end of October or the beginning of November 2018 Rhona began to suffer from increasingly painful legs — specifically the outside of her upper thighs — and started to have trouble walking. After self-medicating with paracetamol the pain was such that codeine was prescribed by a GP which for a short time seemed to help. On the morning of Tuesday November 13th 2018 we paid another visit to the local surgery where the consensus of opinion from two separate GPs was that Rhona had oedema — an accumulation of fluid in her legs, most likely as a result of her failing heart. Having already mentioned the money I'd inherited from my dad's estate, mid-morning on the very same day — November 13th 2018 — I'd had an appointment with my solicitor to make my will, leaving everything to Rhona. This may sound like an unusual thing to do given not only the age difference but the seriousness of Rhona's illnesses, yet in some inexplicable way I'd always felt that I would be the first to go. It's not rational and I don't pretend to be able to explain it in a logical fashion; it was just a feeling that I'd long had (though a naturally melancholic disposition and a fairly uniformly bleak outlook on life and an all-too-keen awareness of its brevity and fragility must play a considerable part), but while everything told me that I should expect that Rhona would quit this mortal coil first I always thought that it would be me. I'd never had anything of substantial value before to leave behind and I thought that now was the time to make my will in Rhona's favour. Be that as it may: following the visit to the surgery Rhona was in considerable discomfort and I didn't want to let her to take me to Hinckley — some eight or nine miles from Blaby — and so immediately after the trip to the doctor we went home for Rhona to rest and I cancelled the solicitor's appointment for another day. Or so I thought. The bitter irony of this is something I've mulled over ever since and will never leave me.

Apart from the quick run up to the surgery this Tuesday was just like every other Tuesday had been for most of the previous three years. Rhona showered and either she or I (I don't remember) prepared the sandwiches which had become the mainstay of her dialysis diet. Certainly I prepared the bag that she took with her — that was always my job — making sure that her blanket, iPhone and iPad (both fully charged), sandwiches and snacks were in it. At four o'clock the car arrived and she limped out to it. Apart from the pain and the awkward hobbling, so far, so normal.

Once again I was wrong to think so.

At around half-past five I was sitting at my desk, writing up my diary for just another ordinary day, when I received a text from Rhona. This was around the time that she would normally be put on dialysis but tonight was different; they were unable to dialyse her because every time the nurses attempted to do so her blood pressure plummeted alarmingly, even dangerously low. To a lesser extent this had always been the case; wide and wild fluctuations in blood pressure — high to low and back again before stabilising — had been a feature of Rhona's dialysis sessions for a long time; problematic but not prohibitive. Now, however, her blood pressure was plummeting too low to allow safe dialysis. After a back-and-forth of text messages and calls between us she told me that it had been decided by the dialysis staff to admit her to Leicester General hospital and an ambulance was sent for. In something of a panic I dashed around the dark streets to the nearest shop with a cashpoint to withdraw some money for a taxi and bought her several puzzle magazines to keep her brain occupied, but later on

Rhona contacted me to say that she had been told by a nurse that there was no point in my going in that evening as visiting hours had ended at eight o'clock. Normally Rhona would have been back home at around half past ten and immediately struggled, panting, up the stairs to bed, but this time I spent a wholly unscheduled, unexpected, unwanted — and anxious — night alone.

The following day however I did get a taxi to the General as soon as I was able; on ward 15N I found Rhona in her hospital bed in a bay at the end of the ward receiving slow but just about adequate dialysis for three hours. She was weak and tired though lucid but above all else in severe pain in her upper legs which paracetamol, tramadol and finally even morphine did little to touch. Two nurses arrived with a scanning machine to conduct a scan of Rhona's heart so I stepped out to buy a sandwich from the hospital shop and to ring Rhona's brother Clive to keep him apprised of the latest news. Back on the ward I stayed with her as long as I was able before phoning for a taxi back to the empty house and a second night alone.

The start of the next day — Thursday — seemed to offer a complete reversal of fortunes. Rhona was out of bed, sitting in the chair next to it, taking nothing stronger than paracetamol and chatting brightly on the phone to me, sounding a thousand times better than the previous evening. She was even planning an attempt at walking; she asked me to bring in the walking frame which had languished, gathering dust, in the garage for the previous three years. Now this, I thought to myself, is the start of Rhona's recovery. The corner has been turned. Rhona is on the mend and I sent borderline jubilant text messages to that effect to various relatives and friends.

I was, yet again, wrong.

Even by the time that I got to the ward at around three o'clock that afternoon things were once again not going well; back in bed Rhona had been attached to a machine designed to rid her of the fluid in her legs and once again her blood pressure kept crashing, to the extent that eventually she was taken off. Rhona had — very quickly it seemed — developed strange, livid, dark red bruise-like marks on her thighs which a group of medical people came to attend to. If it's not part of the morning ward round, a huddle of specialists, doctors and nurses around a patient's bed can never be something to make the average patient or visitor think *oh, that's a good sign.* The decision was taken to move Rhona to a different part of the ward, from 15N to 15A where the more seriously ill are treated. I'm a snivelling coward when it comes to medical things actually being done to me but as a writer I flatter myself that I've picked up a somewhat better than average layman's knowledge of medical matters; yet amid all the technical jargon passing back and forth between one sawbones and another I heard a word which I had never heard before: *calciphylaxis. Calci-* ... well, that's presumably something to do with calcium. *Phylaxis* ... no idea. I'd heard of prophylaxis — preventing an illness — but not calciphylaxis. When the opportunity presented itself I went somewhere quiet further down the ward, pulled out my smartphone and Googled the term.

My stomach dropped into my espadrilles. Calciphylaxis is an extremely serious and highly painful condition in which calcium deposits accumulate in blood vessels near the surface of the skin, causing blood clots, extremely painful ulcers and leaves the sufferer wide open to serious and frequently fatal infections. The prognosis is bleak. Statistically rare in itself, it's a complication seen in a small percentage of patients with end-stage renal failure who have been receiving dialysis for some time; it's more common in women, the obese and those taking medications such as warfarin, vitamin D and calcium supplements — all of which applied to Rhona. Rhona's nephrologist offered the merest glimmer of hope in saying that some people do survive the condition but it was cold comfort: I had already read how seriously are the odds stacked against them. Treatment is little more than supportive and while, yes, a few people do recover, for the great majority the outlook remains frankly grim.

Perhaps it was here more than at any other point where, however faintly, however distantly, the death knell began to sound. I tried to push the dreaded possibility that I would not even mentally name not merely to the back but out of my mind altogether but I knew that the situation had just taken an unforeseen and deeply grave turn for the worse. When the crowd around the bed had dispersed I quietly cornered a young female Asian doctor at the end of the bay — out of Rhona's earshot — and asked what would happen next, though I would not ask or even allow myself to think of asking the question which was fluttering around the edges of my consciousness like a death's head moth. I received the standard, formulaic, indeed the only possible responses. *Please try not to worry. We're doing everything that we possibly can.* What else can they say, or do?

Rhona felt unclean. Behind the curtains around her bed I stripped her and carefully washed her with a grey cardboard bowl of warm water, soap and a flannel before, with considerable difficulty, changing her nightdress and knickers and rubbing ibuprofen gel onto her legs, which given the fact that morphine was barely touching the pain was as good as useless. There was a final tender conversation between us — the last proper exchange we ever had, as it turned out — the details of which I will not record here. I've been consistently honest throughout this account but some things I prefer to hold in memory. Rhona, in pain but drowsy, wanted to get some sleep so I kissed her and left at seven o'clock to get yet another taxi home. I wanted to stay with her and would have been glad to have napped in the chair at her bedside but it wasn't an option held out to me, unfortunately. In the meantime Rhona would be moved from 15N to 15A — the more acute section of the ward. For another time I came back to a house empty save for the dog and the cats, to scrape together something approaching food and go to bed. I would not be gone for long.

Chapter Twelve

Gone in the Morning

> Human relationships are strange. I mean, you are with one person a while, eating and sleeping and living with them, loving them, talking to them, going places together, then it stops.
>
> —Charles Bukowski: *Women*

I can't now recall if I had actually fallen asleep or was just drifting off but at midnight exactly — my mobile phone records the call as coming in at 00:00 — my phone, charging on the bedside drawers, rang. Immediately wide awake I sat bolt upright and answered the phone. It was Rhona, sounding distraught. *Steven, I need you here. I need you to come in and fight for me.*

I leapt out of bed and dragged on my clothes in seconds flat, simultaneously texting *I'm coming dumpling* — the very last ever text message between us out of potentially tens of thousands over our years together. Despite the lateness of the hour my local taxi firm was still running and they got a minicab round to the house within minutes. The dark streets of Leicester were largely empty and the driver, perhaps sensing the urgency of the situation (*who gets a taxi to a hospital after midnight but the truly desperate?* I thought), seriously put his boot down.

I was back at the General and hurrying down its corridors in what can only be described as record time.

Even in the few hours that I'd been off the ward things had gone from very bad to even worse. Under the harsh hospital lights Rhona, still on 15A, was being prepared to be moved to the intensive treatment unit, sitting propped up, conscious albeit still in great pain, and when I arrived being encouraged to drink some sort of glucose drink and eat a spoonful of what I think was yoghurt or caramel or something like it. I can't quite remember. She had low blood sugar which needed to be raised. Even my encouragement, cajoling and pleading couldn't get her to take more than a mouthful. With some of her belongings piled on the bed and others being carried by me, two porters, possibly a doctor and a couple of nurses wheeled Rhona's bed from 15A to the ITU. The General is a low hospital of only two floors but vast in extent; it was a long, a very long walk down one bare, bleak, empty corridor after another until we reached, finally, the ITU at around half-past one in the morning. This was — is — a relatively small high-dependency unit of about half a dozen beds where the most desperately ill patients are cared for on a one-to-one basis by a designated nurse, in Rhona's case a wonderful nurse named Andrea.

For the uninitiated (and that's most of us until we are unfortunate enough to visit one) an ITU is an assault on all the senses. It was a carnival of electronica; beeping, bleeping, flashing machines, wires, plastic tubes, pipes, pumps, bags, antiseptic smells, all the impedimenta of the aggressive medical treatment of the (potentially) mortally ill. I've already said that in medical matters I freely admit that I'm a born coward and am extremely afraid of hospitals; intensive treatment/care units are frightening places to be in and around because the only reason to be in one is because you are or someone you love is dangerously ill. Nobody requires intensive care for sore piles or an itchy groin.

After a little while with Rhona I was shown into a small visitor's room further down the corridor while the necessary ministrations were carried out. This happened several more times in the few hours that I was there. It was a (presumably) purposely bland, pastel, anonymous room with sun- and age-faded art on the walls; a box room for visitors to sleep in, to wait in and, as I was soon to discover, to hear the worst news of their lives in and have their lives shattered in. With very good reason Simon Thomas in his memoir *Love, Interrupted* refers to these places as the 'room of doom'; Maddy Paxman in *The Great Below* calls them the Bad News Room. Both terms are only too apt. Every hospital should have one. In fact I dare say that every hospital does. I suppose I sat and looked at the wall until somebody — I can't remember who; it may have been Andrea or it may have been someone else — came in and said that I could come back onto the ITU. Rhona had been connected to sundry machinery; she had what I always think of as the American-style oxygen tubing in her nostrils rather than a face mask. Her chest seemed to be a mass of wires and tubes leading to machines on stands next to her bed with coloured flashing numbers and lights. I was predictably aghast and tried not to show myself to be so. Rhona was awake albeit drowsy; I remained with her until five o'clock in the morning when I left to let her get some sleep. Once again, if staying with her had been an option I would certainly have done so (if only ...) but it wasn't; given that this was a high-dependency unit visitors, unavoidably, can tend to get in the way. I got another taxi back to a silent house and went to bed.

Another day dawned; Friday November 16th 2018. It would be the last full day of Rhona's life. I didn't know this and I've wondered ever since how I would have reacted had I known that fact beforehand. As soon as visiting hours began at eleven o'clock I called the ward; I was told that the doctors, doing their daily ward round, had literally just arrived at Rhona's bed and was asked to call back later. Physically, mentally, emotionally exhausted and fogged by Valium I must have been in a dazed state; it's hard to believe these days but I cooked and ate a Waitrose vegan pizza while I was dumbly watching the American remake of the Japanese horror film *The Ring* — bizarre, the trivial, footling, inconsequential details that stick in the memory when other, far more important things are a blank — and called again. Rhona's designated nurse quietly told me that a Dr Bell wanted me to come onto the ward for 'a chat'. My stomach lurched. Being asked to go into hospital for 'a chat' with a doctor is never good news. Frantically I downed a

Valium to smother a rising sense of panic and booked a taxi, arriving back on the ITU at around 1:20pm.

On the ward a serious but sympathetic Andrea introduced me to an absurdly young-looking Dr Bell. The old adage is that you know that you begin to feel old when the policemen start to look young, but given zero experience with policemen and extensive experience with hospitals I find that it's more true of doctors; when highly trained, highly qualified and massively experienced medical experts are the best part of two decades younger than you decrepitude raises its head. The three of us went to the room of doom and sat down, Andrea and Dr Bell sitting across from me — two against one, as it felt. Dulled by Valium I steeled myself as much as I was able. *I have to tell you that Rhona is very seriously ill*, Dr Bell said, *but we're doing everything for her that we possibly can*. I suppose I nodded dumbly. *They're doing all that they can*, I said to myself. *Of course they are. That's what they're for. That's what they do. They're doing all they can.*

David had already been alerted to the terrible news; he had formerly lived in Florida but had relatively recently moved close to Seattle on the other side of the continental United States and therefore had that much further to travel. Frantically he tried to get the earliest possible flight over to Britain. Mid-afternoon Leah arrived at the hospital from her home in Derbyshire, followed later on by her wife Claire; we met up in the hospital's café. This was barely two or three hours since I had arrived on the ITU but even in that short space of time the situation had changed disastrously; any flame of hope no matter how slight or faint was now decisively extinguished. The Bad News Room lived up to its name; a sombre Dr Bell quietly told me and Leah that Rhona had deteriorated so significantly and so quickly that there was now no hope that she could survive. It may take hours, possibly a day or even two, but Rhona's heart was failing her and there was no possibility that that state of affairs could be reversed. She was going to die.

There isn't really any simple or straightforward way of writing about how one receives news of that kind. I know that I was pacified by diazepam and was therefore, to a certain extent at least, insulated from the full horror of the news. Because it's a tranquiliser Valium, like alcohol or some other drugs I would imagine, is akin to a car's airbag; it cushions you against impact. What it must be like for people not so insulated I can't begin to imagine.

Leah, Claire and I went back to the ITU and joined Rhona, who was now semi-conscious and fading away even from that. With the curtains drawn around the bed I took a seat on Rhona's right-hand side, holding her right hand as I would do to the end hours later, not moving, occasionally kissing it. Rhona's long-time nephrologist appeared on the ward and in a harrowing conversation held out the glimmer of hope that it has been known for people to recover from calciphylaxis; but for one thing I had already read too much to know that while technically true the chances of this were vanishingly slim, and for another, this was no longer just about calciphylaxis. This was not kidney failure but heart failure. I confess to a selfish and unworthy thought that shows me in a bad light (again): I wish I had been alone with Rhona. I wish that it had just been the two of us as it had been for so much of our union, especially the latter part of it during her illness. She was going to die and I knew it and I wanted to be the last one — the only one — to say goodbye to her. *Why can't it just be me and Rhona? It's always been just me and Rhona. Why can't it just be me and Rhona? Why are they here? It should just be me and Rhona.* Horribly, I resented the fact that fact that Rhona's death had to be shared, even with her own daughter and daughter-in-law. I wanted Rhona all to myself in her dying even as I wanted her all to myself in life. *Nobody else; just you and me, Wo.* Ugly thoughts, no question, but there at the time and I can only relate the honest facts.

Machines monitored Rhona's vital signs: heart rate, blood pressure, oxygen saturation, much more that I didn't and don't understand. Beep, beep, beep, beep, beep, beep, beep. Heart rate. Pulse. Blood pressure. Oxygen. Heart rate. Pulse. Blood pressure. Oxygen. Heart rate. Pulse. Blood pressure. Oxygen. Coloured flashing numbers, coloured lines tracking across screens, on expensive and complicated, largely incomprehensible-save-to-the-initiated medical machines. Beep, beep, beep. The final electronic noises of the modern way of death.

Time passed … somehow. We were told that Rhona had been, Rhona *was* receiving the largest possible doses of medication to raise her blood pressure that human beings can take. It wasn't working. We were informed that with nothing further to be done it had been decided that treatment, aside from pain relief, would be withdrawn. Rhona was going to die, and soon. Then came the inevitable question that no doctor wants to hear or have to answer. *How long, doctor?* We received the same response as before. It might be a matter of hours, it might even be a day, nobody could possibly say. But nevertheless, she was certainly going to die. Soon.

Treatment, now hopeless apart from pain relief, was stopped at about half past eight, half an hour after the handover of day to night staff. Leah, Claire and I continued to sit at Rhona's bedside, dumbly awaiting the inevitable, counting the hours, letting minute by minute by minute pass, keeping the vigil while the activity of the rest of the ITU swirled around us just beyond the curtains. What had until the afternoon been a hospital visit now became that most surreal of human experiences, a deathwatch. As Joyce Carol Oates writes in *A Widow's Story*:

> There are two categories of hospital vigils.
> The vigil with the happy ending, and the other.
> Embarked upon the hospital vigil as in a small canoe on a churning white-water river you can have no clear idea which vigil you are embarked upon—until it has come to an end.
> Until the patient has been discharged from the hospital and brought safely home. Or not discharged, and never brought home.

Minutes, then hours passed, my eyes fixed on the monitors next to the bed with their flashing multicoloured numbers and jagged lines of declining life: heart rate, blood pressure, oxygen saturation, other things that I didn't and don't comprehend, the full panoply of modern medicine. Flashing numbers in different colours, spiky lines tracking left to right (or vice versa? I don't remember), beeps and bleeps and alarms. Partly due to Valium, partly to incredible physical and emotional exhaustion, partly to anticipatory grief, the situation at times felt unreal, dreamlike. I was undeniably there, but also not there.

The minutes passed and became hours. I clung to Rhona's right hand, Leah to her left. The machines flashed, beeped and bleeped. Occasionally a nurse would appear through the curtains to check the monitors; to check on Rhona; to check on us as well, I imagine. I suppose almost inevitably, this being Britain, tea was offered though not as far as I'm aware taken up. I don't think so. I don't know. I don't remember.

It was at about five minutes to eleven that Rhona's already damaged heart began to fail. Rhona had long since lapsed into unconsciousness, but, though I am no medical man, I don't believe that she was in a coma at least as I understand the term; she was unconscious but not comatose, not unresponsive — as far as I'm able to tell. As I say I'm no medical men and may be wrong. With half-lidded eyes she was still swallowing saliva. Pain relief was still being administered but I didn't believe then and don't believe now that she experienced any discomfort at any stage; she was too far gone for that. She simply ebbed away.

Nevertheless it was the beginning of the end.

In extremis the helplessness of grief and sorrow can make us banal, trivial. At one point during this process, thinking that Rhona, with a hospital blanket laid over the sheets, was still sufficiently aware to hear and to know my voice I said: "Are you warm enough, Wo?" Her head nodded up and down by a minute amount, an incredibly small, almost imperceptible lift and fall of her chin. I don't know, I will never now know, whether this was an entirely coincidental reflex action or whether it was a barely conscious positive response to my question. Was she aware just enough — just enough; just sufficiently — to respond, or was it an incidental physical reaction? Was it the last communication of sorts from the love of my life to me? *Yes I'm warm enough, thanks.* Or was it merely an involuntary movement? As I say, I will never know. I keep asking the question to which I know there can never be an answer.

From the time that her heart function began to falter it took Rhona two hours to die. There were no heroics and no dramatics, just intermittent bouts of weeping from the vigil-keepers. It was a slow, quiet and gentle winding down, as with a watch or clock that slowly loses kinetic energy and eventually comes to a stop. Rhona's death followed the pattern of her final illness; the opposite of something like, for example, cancer — an active and aggressive disease — it was a passive procedure, a happening-to rather than a being-done-to. There were no deathbed traumas, just a gentle fading away. A slow death; a quiet death; a peaceful death; a gentle death. In *Why Not Me?* Barbara Want writes that death can be brutal but it can also be beautiful. I don't buy it; I'm not at all sure I can agree that there can be anything beautiful about any death, certainly not of someone you love and least of all the death of the person you love most in the world. But I'll concede that there are definitely better and worse ways to die and Rhona's — thank whatever gods may be — was one of the better ones. Life gently ebbing away; sleeping away; going away. 'Fell asleep', found on so many old tombstones, is as much of a euphemism as is 'passed away' but is in this case accurate. Rhona fell asleep. There would have been one final breath and then no more: the end.

The only thing that mattered then and matters now, and will always matter, is that I was there. At the age of forty-six I had seen two human beings breathe their last in my presence. As it happened both deaths were of the two most important people (let alone women) in my life; my mum in August 2001 and now Rhona. In *Grief Works* Julia Samuel observes that people die as they have lived — a statement which manages to be simultaneously profound and an expression of the bleeding obvious, and I'd imagine not necessarily even always true. Calm, peaceful, gentle people can sometimes (though not always) die calmly, gently and peacefully. Angry, difficult and adversarial people can (though not always) die angrily. In my two experiences, quiet, gentle souls died quiet and gentle deaths.

At five minutes to one in the morning of Saturday November 17th 2018 a short, stout, far-Eastern nurse appeared through the curtains around Rhona's bed and gently said to us: "She's gone." On the monitors there was, as I recalled from my mum's death seventeen years earlier, some residual electrical cardiac activity, but this is normal and essentially

Rhona was indeed gone. After very close to twenty-one years together — all but a few weeks — Rhona, at the age of sixty-seven, was dead.

She had been ill for three and a half years and at the end in hospital a little over three days.

It was the first hour of another Saturday. In a few hours the city of Leicester would awaken to a new day that Rhona would never see; traffic would flow along its busy roads, post would be delivered, breakfasts eaten, showers taken, teeth brushed, the minutiae of normal everyday life. Some people at least would awaken to another working day; children to be roused, washed, dressed and fed; weekend activities to be planned. Ten days before her death Rhona (on her borrowed mobility scooter) and I had been on a shopping expedition where I had bought a few new items of clothing, as ever carefully appraised by madam herself. A few days beforehand Rhona had still been driving and shopping and sending parcels in the post office. At the beginning of the week she had as usual been glued to her iPad, taking photographs and listing stock on eBay, making sandwiches and watching *Bargain Hunt* as usual. Now she was gone for ever.

The three of us were shown back into the room of doom down the corridor while the staff busied themselves with removing the visible signs of the heroic medical efforts made to keep Rhona alive and then, when that was no longer an option, to make and keep her comfortable. We were given blankets; the light was turned out; on too-small couches we tried to sleep for an unknown period of time. I am six foot three and tried to sleep on a couch seemingly made for a midget, head on one armrest and legs hanging over the edge of the other. Despite the Valium and the unbelievable exhaustion I don't think I truly slept; a shallow half-in, half-out doze from time to time was as much as I could manage.

Eventually, at about twenty minutes to three, we were summoned back onto the unit where Rhona now lay in her bed divested of all tubes, wires and every other kind of equipment with which she had been covered. She was — obviously — perfectly still and looked perfectly peaceful, as though she was merely enjoying the soundest possible sleep … which she now was. In tears I kissed her cooling forehead and then, finally, the right hand which I had held in life and had clung to so tightly in the final hours of that life. Leah and Claire said their farewells on the other side of the bed. The last goodbyes to Rhona's physical form had been said. By definition ITU staff must see death and have to deal with the immediately bereaved almost every day and are therefore professionally kind but not feignedly so; they were wonderfully compassionate. They may be well versed in it all but daily they don't pretend; they see people in the worst extremity of emotional pain and (usually) know how to manage it.

Rhona died one day before what would have been her forty-second wedding anniversary with John, had he lived (and one day short of eighteen years since we had moved into the house in Wareham Road). In actuality they were together for something over twenty years; coincidentally so were we. She died not quite a month before what would have been our own twenty-first anniversary or anniversaries, unofficial as they were.

For years Rhona and I had worn matching rings, clearly not wedding rings so let's call them commitment or promise rings; not at all expensive in monetary terms, if anything quite cheap, but in terms of sentimental value utterly priceless beyond any figure you may care to name. Rhona's ring along with all her other personal effects were handed over by hospital staff; Leah gave it to me and it hangs on a chain around my neck alongside the Star of David that Rhona bought for me in the earliest days of our relationship. My ring remains on my finger. All will stay there until they are similarly removed.

Like saucer-eyed shell-shocked soldiers, dim, dumb and dazed with grief and utter exhaustion (and in my case tranquilisers) we left a largely silent and empty hospital at about three o'clock in the morning. Leah and Claire took me back to Blaby and dropped me off at the house at around twenty past three. After letting the dog into the garden I went upstairs, undressed and fell into bed, too exhausted in all ways, too dull-headed by multiple doses of Valium, too stunned by the immediacy and the enormity of my loss, to realise that when I awoke to daylight again — it would be a bright, brilliant, blue-skied early winter's day of which I remember nothing save that it was rounded off by a breath-taking sunset — I would, after close to twenty-one years, be starting my new life as a widower.

Part Two

The Absence – Without

Chapter Thirteen

Heartbreak in the Heart of Things

> This is what those who haven't crossed the tropic of grief often fail to understand: the fact that someone is dead may mean that they are not alive, but doesn't mean that they do not exist.
>
> —Julian Barnes: *Levels of Life*

I have little to no memory of the first few days after Rhona's death. Valium is known to interfere with the formation of short-term memories, but then so do shock, grief and exhaustion and I was immersed in all four of these. I was in shock and probably unable to process well very much of anything very much. My sole memory of the day of Rhona's death is that it ended with a glorious, blazing autumn-winter sunset (early in mid-November, of course) over the golf course near our house, seen dumbly by me when I took Tilly out for a walk just as it had been seen by me times beyond number in all those years beforehand when I would return to the house — dog lead in hand, shoes off at the front door, coat off and thrown onto the newel post at the bottom of the stairs — to find Rhona there and now would not and would never do so again.

I do know that within three days of Rhona's death I began to come down with what turned out to be one of the worst colds I've ever had in my life which hit me like an express train and took a long time to get over, possibly the longest I've ever known. I needn't have been surprised; while it could of course have been purely coincidental, to my mind it seems far more probable that the stress of the previous week had given my immune system such a serious and severe knock that I was laid wide open to any passing bug. I spent several days of abject wretchedness in bed, worrying Leah to the extent that when she called round to the house and took one look at me she offered to get a doctor to make a house call, which I refused. Doctors have far more on their plate than to visit people laid up in bed with a cold, however bad it may be. There were more days just about upright but dragging myself around the house like a very old man, sweating and groaning and feeling as though I had fallen downstairs, been beaten to a pulp when I got there and then been run over by a tank.

There is more than enough evidence (and has been for a long time) to tell us that the recently bereaved have significantly higher mortality rates than the rest of the population. It is not simply a question of the newly bereft killing themselves, though that of course does sometimes happen (and frankly I'm surprised that it doesn't occur more often than it does): it really does seem that profound and protracted grief damages people so deeply and so badly that they are not only at higher risk of accidents but that their own bodies turn traitor. In *The Long Goodbye* Meghan O'Rourke observes:

> Not surprisingly, perhaps, the clinical literature on grief is extensive. Much of it reinforces what I had already begun to realize. Grief isn't rational; it isn't linear; it is experienced in waves. "No one ever told me that grief felt so like fear," C. S. Lewis had written at the beginning of *A Grief Observed*, and scientists have in fact found that grief, like fear, is a stress reaction, attended by deep physiological changes. Levels of stress hormones like cortisol increase. Sleep patterns are disrupted. The immune system is weakened. Mourners may experience loss of appetite, palpitations, even hallucinations. Just

> as I had, they sometimes imagine that the deceased has appeared to them, in the form of a bird, say, or a cat [...] Freud theorized that the reason for all this distress has to do with energy. In his essay 'Mourning and Melancholia', he suggests that mourners have to reclaim the energy they have invested in the deceased loved ones. Grieving is that process of reclamation.

Suicides happen; clumsiness increases and accidents large and small occur, as evidenced by Jonathan Santlofer in *The Widower's Notebook*:

> Since Joy died I have dropped a heavy wooden painting panel on my foot, which fractured several bones. I have tripped, hit my head on a table, and knocked myself unconscious, awakened seconds or possibly minutes later, with my face in a pool of blood, nose broken and forehead lacerated, which later needed stitches in my eyebrow, and embedded glass taken out of my lip. Not long after that, I slid on wet leaves running to the subway, twisted my foot, and tore ligaments.

There were other, minor accidents, a badly cut finger, another less serious fall. There were two bouts of a serious backache [...] There are also the continuing eye issues.

And the migraines.

People succumb to illnesses, some grave, some ostensibly almost trivial; months after Rhona's death my own health broke down. The fact, backed up by abundant research, is that for a variety of reasons — some known, some mysterious — deep grief can and does not merely harm but may kill. In *Grieving: A Beginner's Guide* Jerusha Hall McCormack states it about as bluntly as it can be put: "The grieving stand at the centre of an experience so intense, it can (and sometimes does) kill them." It is, we now know, entirely possible to die of what is conventionally known as a broken heart. Aside from the romantic Hollywood notions of dying for love and/or grief we know that severe and immediate stress can sometimes cause serious but temporary illness and can, in certain cases, also prove lethal. What's popularly known as broken heart syndrome is a usually transient heart condition brought about by acute stress, caused by a very abrupt and colossal surge of stress hormones such as adrenaline and cortisol — not only the death of a loved one but the loss of a job, the announcement of divorce, even a very heated argument can bring it about. Fundamentally, any source of sudden and severe emotional upheaval can cause it. While broken heart syndrome has a certain ring for the layman it's more formally known as apical ballooning syndrome, stress-induced cardiomyopathy or takotsubo cardiomyopathy, *takotsubo* being the Japanese word for a particular kind of octopus trap whose shape mirrors the bulging balloon of the heart's left ventricle. (The name has stuck because while known as a phenomenon since the year dot the first scientifically-reported cases began to appear in Japan in the early 1990s). It is non-ischaemic — in other words not a 'heart attack' as popularly understood — but at first sight the symptoms mimic one; central chest pain, shortness of breath, clamminess and so forth, although examination doesn't reveal the sort of arterial blockage associated with a true heart attack. Most people make a full recovery within a few days or weeks and experience no further problems (though it can recur if the initial source of stress persists) but in certain cases the condition can prove fatal — a small minority of people can and do go on to develop congestive heart failure and/or severe hypotension to which they succumb.

Takotsubo cardiomyopathy disguises itself as a heart attack, but additional research has demonstrated that the grieving are at serious risk of what we might call the genuine article. Dr Murray Mittelman, a cardiologist and epidemiologist at Harvard Medical School, has stated that: "Caretakers, healthcare providers and the bereaved themselves need to recognise they are in a period of heightened risk in the days and weeks after hearing of someone close dying." Researchers interviewed patients who had had had a confirmed heart attack between 1989 and 1994; part of the research involved asking them about the circumstances leading up to their heart attack including whether they had recently experienced the death of someone very close to them. The results demonstrated that those who had recently lost a significant and important figure in their lives had a risk of heart attack twenty-one times higher than normal within the first day of being bereaved and still six times higher than normal within the first week. Grieving spouses are particularly at peril; cardiovascular disease — heart attacks and strokes — accounts for as many as 53% of deaths.

It's not merely cardiac complications from which the bereaved are at danger. As reported in the *Telegraph* in March 2012, immunological research at the University of Birmingham headed by Professor Janet Lord concluded that the severe systemic shock of grief can so badly compromise the body's immune response, especially in the elderly, that death may ensue. Citing the examples of country legend Johnny Cash who succumbed to complications of diabetes in 2003 four months after losing his adored wife June and former Prime Minister James Callaghan who died a mere ten days after his wife of sixty-seven years, the article reveals that the drastically increased stress levels as found in the wake of the death of a loved one interfere with the production of a type of white blood cell known as a neutrophil which are known to play an important role in fighting bacterial infections such as the pneumonia which killed Lord Callaghan. The elderly are particularly at risk because while young people produce another hormone known as DHEAS (dehydroepiandrosterone) which has a buffering effect against infection, the ability to produce DHEAS drops off with age; a seventy year-old has only 10 to 20% of the DHEAS of a thirty year-old, so those in the older age groups are drastically less well protected than the young.

The Birmingham University research was based on a sample of forty-eight adults over the age of sixty-five; half the group had suffered a major bereavement in the preceding three months while the other half had not. Examination of the immune systems of the sample group found that the antibacterial protection of neutrophils was significantly reduced in those who had been bereaved when compared to those who had not, a condition known as neutropenia. They had — fairly obviously one might have thought — raised levels of stress hormones such as cortisol which suppresses the action of neutrophils. "There are a lot of anecdotes about couples who were married for forty years when one of them passes away and the other dies a few days later," said Professor Lord. "It seems there is a biological basis for this. Rather than dying of a broken heart [...] they are dying of a broken immune system. They usually get infections [...] Our results in healthy adults who have suffered bereavement show the effect on the immune system of this stress is as profound as we saw in those who had suffered a hip fracture. We think that what is going on is that even previously healthy people are becoming very depressed and this has a powerful effect [...] Treating depression after bereavement [...] may therefore help older adults to recover and avoid life-threatening infections." This is no longer the stuff of legends, anecdote, pulp novels and equally pulpy movies; the hard science is in — grief kills.

And then in the absence of these known causes of death are the mysterious — because still unexplained by medical science — deaths of the bereaved (often, though by no means exclusively, spouses) which occur for no known reason, as though their own life force simply ebbs, drains away until there is none left to sustain existence. Many people can dredge up a heard or half-heard anecdote of the kind referred to by Professor Lord of the elderly, long-married couple one of whom dies only to be followed into the dark by their mate only months, weeks or even days later. Hence the famously pithy seventeenth-century epigram by Sir Henry Wotton, 'Upon the Death of Sir Albert Morton's Wife':

> He first deceased; she for a little tried
> To live without him, liked it not, and died.

David, his wife and infant son arrived from the States, staying at a nearby hotel. While I was enduring the mother of all colds practical matters had to be attended to. That inevitably meant arranging what we variously called the funeral but at other times the memorial service because the service proper and the burial were two separate events on two consecutive days eighty miles apart. I had always known and fully accepted that, being a widow when we met, Rhona had made her wish clear to be laid to rest in the grave of her late husband at the Weston Road cemetery in the northern part of Stevenage. Buried, not cremated — this is in accordance with Jewish tradition; observant Jews are buried as quickly as possible after death and cremation is forbidden — though was not chosen for that reason, I think. She had stipulated as much in her will. I had always been perfectly fine with this plan and understood entirely its rationale but in practical terms it meant that the torture of her funeral was prolonged, extended to two days rather than just one. Whether it's a burial or — far more prevalent these days — a cremation, for the vast majority of us a funeral means maybe an hour at the crematorium, possibly in a church or other place of worship, and that is very much that: the mourners eventually disperse and the funeral directors go behind the scenes to do what funeral directors do. In Rhona's case however her send-off was stretched out over two days: a large memorial service at the local crematorium followed by a much smaller, quieter, private burial attended by close family only in Stevenage the following day.

On the Monday following Rhona's death David, Leah, Claire and I went into Leicester to begin the process of attending to the formalities. Green, official-looking paperwork had to be collected from the General hospital; the death had to be registered and a death certificate issued by a registrar in a sunlit room with too few chairs; back in Blaby as night fell we made an appointment for the following day with a local funeral director (and a particularly well-known company at that). With Valium still swirling around my system I leadenly watched much of this flow past and around me rather than through me, wanting to be involved but not wanting to intrude or to be thought of as intruding in the presence of Rhona's children.

The next day we arrived at the funeral director's at the appointed time to arrange the funeral-cum-memorial service, leafing through brochures of coffins as though it was an Argos catalogue. Incredible as it now seems I was dulled by so much Valium that placidly I went along with choosing a light oak coffin — the Chatsworth model, rather appropriate in a way since a few years earlier Rhona and I had had a short break in Derbyshire and had visited Chatsworth House. We were asked: *what would you like Rhona to be buried in?* For years Rhona had had a once-yearly and specific Christmas Day outfit, a black sweater and skirt with Christmas tree lights and baubles on it; we decided that she would be buried in this outfit — a mordant touch of humour in an otherwise bleak experience. A funeral notice was prepared for the local paper:

> Rhona Sonia Shafik passed away peacefully following a long illness on Saturday November 17th 2018 aged 67. Loving daughter of Zena and sister to Clive, adored mum of Leah and David, loving mum-in-law to Claire and Frances, adoring grandma to Gabriel and beloved partner of Steve. Memorial service to be held at South Leicestershire Crematorium, Foston Road, Countesthorpe, Leicestershire, LE8 5QP at 4:00 p.m. on Tuesday December 4th 2018. Instead of flowers the family welcome donations to Kidney Research UK, the British Heart Foundation and the Leicester Hospitals Charity.

Aside from long ago having made her wish known to be buried with John in Stevenage Rhona had left behind no directions or instructions for her funeral so some of what we did can be classed under the heading of winging it. (Though not a great deal, not when you know someone sufficiently well and closely to know their like and dislikes, preferences and interests). Culturally Jewish but non-religious as Rhona was we selected a non-religious funeral celebrant (curious title), the very same one who had conducted my dad's funeral only eight months previously, who called at the house a few days later. I recall that even at the time, as she sat on the couch gathering details, stories and anecdotes about Rhona to form the basis of her eulogy, I reflected on the irony (if that's what it is) that only eight months earlier Rhona and I had sat with her doing precisely the same about dad, and now here I was haltingly doing the same for Rhona.

David and Leah, by definition being of a different generation to their quondam free-wheeling hippy-dippy free spirit child-of-the-Sixties mum, were stumped for the choice of two pieces of entry-and-exit music and left it up to me. This was one of the easiest parts of the process: I chose David Bowie's 'Kooks' for Rhona's favourite line about a lover's story and 'In My Life' by The Beatles for the poignancy and accuracy of its lyrics. In my view and experience truly excellent poetry about grief, bereavement and mourning suitable for public rather than solitary reading is comparatively rare so we opted for a very common but poignant choice, 'She Is Gone' by David Harkins:

You can shed tears that she is gone
or you can smile because she has lived.

You can close your eyes and pray that she'll come back
or you can open your eyes and see all that she's left.

Your heart can be empty because you can't see her
or you can be full of the love you shared.

You can turn your back on tomorrow and live yesterday
or you can be happy for tomorrow because of yesterday.

You can remember her and only that she's gone
or you can cherish her memory and let it live on.

You can cry and close your mind,
be empty and turn your back,
or you can do what she'd want:
smile, open your eyes, love and go on.
(© David Harkins)

Over the next few days we prepared a printed order of service containing photographs from various stages of Rhona's life — a young Rhona with John; Rhona with baby David and infant Leah; Rhona and me — and the text of 'She Is Gone'.

The opportunity was extended to see Rhona for the final time in the 'Chapel of Rest'. (How many euphemisms we hedge around death to soften the knife edges ...). I refused (as did everyone else) and knew that I was making absolutely the right decision. I had similarly refused the offer to see my mum back in 2001 and have never regretted it for a millisecond. Everybody is different and doubtless some people find it emotionally and psychologically useful to see their dead loved one insofar as it helps them to admit the reality of death. More power to them, but though the causes were different the circumstances of my mum's death and that of Rhona were almost identical; I was present at the bedside in intensive care units, holding their hands in both cases, and my last sight of the both of them was immediately after death, still pink, still warm and looking no more than soundly asleep as they might have been lying in bed at home. I wanted to keep it that way. When an uncle died in 2002 his sister — my aunt Joan — decided that she wanted to see him at the local funeral director's and although I personally had absolutely no desire to see him I volunteered to accompany her. It was, as far as I was and am concerned, a colossal mistake; in his coffin he looked pale, slightly yellow and waxy like one of Madame Tussaud's less successful creations, oddly shrunken — collapsed; caved in; *diminished* — and not quite real. I certainly was not going to experience anything of that nature with my mum and definitely not with Rhona either. Some of the bereavement books I've read actively recommend that people see the body before burial or cremation, which seems to me to be entirely wrong-headed advice. People decide these things for themselves, of course, but in the two most important and shattering deaths in my lifetime I opted not to do so and in both cases I was absolutely right not to.

Tuesday December 4th 2018 — a short, grey winter day, the day of Rhona's memorial service-cum-funeral — arrived. Due to the amount of diazepam I needed to get through the experience I remember relatively little of it. I am still undecided if that's a curse or a blessing.

As with so much else I may never have a final answer to this.

People began to arrive at the house. In the afternoon I showered, shaved and dressed in the crisp white shirt and mourning black suit, tie and shiny black shoes I had dragged down from the loft a few days before, not touched — not needed to be touched — since my dad's funeral several months earlier. I recall looking forward to the time when I knew that I could load myself up with the largest dose of Valium I had and have ever taken at any one time in my life — 40mg — to pacify me through the ordeal.

Caterers, arranged by Rhona's brother Clive, arrived at the house laden with goodies; they did their thing in the kitchen and in the dining room while the rest of us sat or stood or paced and awaited the inevitable. Dumb, dulled and dimmed by prescription drugs I saw shiny black funeral cars glide slowly like whales into our cul-de-sac and I found myself climbing into one such, the black-garbed professionally mournful opening and closing the car door for me. Fortunately the crematorium, opened only three years earlier, was a short ride away, probably no more than a couple of miles at the very most, a spartan, utilitarian building, bare, white, minimalist. They had not bothered to take down the large cross hanging on the wall which I had believed to be standard practice when it's known that someone is not a practising Christian. Incongruous, inappropriate even, but I was in no position to raise any objection.

Heavily medicated as I was, arriving at the crem is mostly lost to me. Much of the experience is. As a very much loved woman with a small family, a relatively small circle of close friends but a very wide circle of acquaintances, attendance was enormous, with mourners coming from far and wide, across all circles of Rhona's personal and professional life. The crematorium was packed out — a full house. Family entered first, followed by friends and then everybody else who had come to pay their respects. The turnout from Rhona's life in beauty pageants was tremendous. To the tune of David Bowie's 'Kooks' and its lover's story men and women in black filed into the crematorium, immediate family at the front, friends and others following in procession. Me, David, Leah, Zena, Clive at the front — the worst possible position for someone like me but inevitable. People took a pew, so to speak. A large and beautiful photograph of a beaming Rhona, the same photograph as on the cover of the order of service, stood on an easel at the front of the room in front of the coffin. The funeral celebrant read, eloquently, the eulogy which we had collectively prepared. I have to admit that I always used to cringe slightly whenever I heard people refer to a funeral as a 'celebration of a life' — to me it always smacked a little too much of clichéd, unimaginative choices in funeral music such as 'My Way' and 'Always Look on the Bright Side of Life' — but now I'm not so sure; Rhona's life was indeed celebrated. There were some flashes of light humour which raised smiles and even laughter from members of the congregation. At various points, although somehow still conscious of multiple pairs of eyes on the back of my head and black suit jacket, I bent forward and wept, silently but copiously. David put his arm around my shuddering shoulders. The most scalding tears came near the end when the music system played the closing song, the Beatles' 'In My Life' — chosen by me with very good reason but frankly a song I hope never to hear again as long as I live. I looked to my left and saw Clive similarly wiping his bespectacled eyes, in a flood of tears for the same reasons.

Things have a beginning, a middle and an end; the memorial service concluded and everybody filed out. There was a crushed gathering of the huge crowd in the space at the rear (or the front) of the crematorium. Old friends of Rhona's — including some people I knew well, relatively well, fairly well, slightly, hardly at all, not at all — came to me to offer their condolences. Numb, I shook hands, exchanged polite pleasantries and commiserations with numerous people, some of whom I had not seen in years or barely knew. Mentally I was barely present and emotionally I was far, far away, but I hope I acquitted myself more or less coherently.

Now in early winter darkness many of the attendees went back to the house, and a singularly packed house never before seen at that. Finger food had been laid on by the excellent caterers; I have absolutely no idea why but I surprised myself by eating unusually well, the first solid nourishment worthy of the name I had had in many days. There was the variously friendly, variously awkward small talk to be found at any wake. People milled around the house, ate and drank — tea and coffee and possibly soft drinks; alcohol had not been provided for, probably wisely in my case because I would have been tempted beyond endurance to imbibe which would likely have killed me — and reminisced about Rhona. Jacketless, I moved through the throng — an unusual house full of people, old friends and complete strangers — in a Valium-induced daze and haze, talking quietly to various relatives and friends. The atmosphere was quiet though not solemn or sombre.

The caterers, who had done such a sterling job, cleaned and cleared up and left. Eventually people began to drift away in their twos and threes, saying their goodbyes and reiterating their condolences. Many had travelled long distances and faced a lengthy return journey through the evening to sundry and in some cases far-flung parts of Britain. I don't remember much of it. At some point later on everybody had left and I was once again alone. At some point I closed the front door on the last to go and at some point the house was silent; me, Tilly, cats … that's it. At some point I undressed; at some point I carefully hung up my black suit for the burial the following day before at some point going to bed and, I assume on account of the medication, sleeping soundly. As I have been at pains to say, I don't remember very much of it.

If I recall correctly by the time of Rhona's death, at the age of forty-six, I had been to five funerals — almost all close relatives, including both of my parents — and all had been relatively short, simple and uncomplicated affairs, all cremations. Now I was presented with the, by now, relatively uncommon prospect of the burial of a coffin. Made legal in 1884, cremation grew incrementally until in 1968 cremations overtook burials; by 2016 three quarters of people were cremated as opposed to buried. This is driven by their own wishes; an August 2016 YouGov poll found that 58% of people would prefer cremation (as do I) when they die as compared to a mere 17% who would prefer burial. (The remaining quarter were presumably undecided). All of my prior funerals had been simple services at a crematorium; now I was faced, within hailing distance of the age of fifty, not only with encountering my first burial of a coffin in the earth but with that coffin bearing the body of the love of my life.

The following day — Wednesday December 5th — was suitably dismal for Rhona's burial; a stereotypically bleak, grey, wind-racked and rain-lashed December day, a wintry, funereal day if ever there was one. I was picked up and driven down to Stevenage by Leah and her wife. Loaded up on Valium for a second day running I sat mostly mute in the back of the car, occasionally weeping. Even numbed by tranquilisers the sight of Stevenage again after eighteen years and so many once-familiar sights including Archer Road — where Rhona and I had started our life together — was an excruciating experience. *This used to be my home. This used to be my life. With Rhona. Rhona who used to be alive and now isn't. Rhona who is about to be buried. How can this be? How can this happen?*

At Weston Road cemetery we met up with the small party of others — there were only around ten of us in total — and walked across sodden grass trodden to sludge to where John's and now Rhona's open grave awaited. A hole in the ground where the love of my life, my soulmate, was about to be deposited, something I had only ever seen before on television. An ashen Clive and a frail Zena arrived to bury their sister and daughter respectively, an ordeal which I can't even begin to imagine. I thought I had it bad. The funeral directors brought Rhona's coffin from the hearse to the grave, at which point I decided that I had already seen very much more than enough, looking to my right at the dark high trees at the cemetery's edge swaying in the frigid wind and keeping my eyes fixed intently on them throughout. I had no desire to watch the procedure. It was my first and only burial and I still didn't see it. At the conclusion Clive handed round sheets of paper, printed copies of the Burial Kaddish for us, Jewish or not, to follow. I was in no position to follow it and offered only a heartfelt if mumbled 'amen' at the end.

The group dispersed to their separate cars. After the burial there was a second gathering — another wake of sorts — at the Cromwell Hotel in the Old Town; not a sombre or subdued affair, there was quiet conversation and even some laughter as we remembered Rhona over sandwiches, cakes and hot drinks, but as with the previous day, people had come a long way and needed to get home at a reasonable time. Leah and her wife brought me back north on a busy, rush hour-packed motorway in pouring rain, dropping me off at the empty house, before continuing to their own home. I closed the front door on a foul night. In her Christmas outfit Rhona was in the ground eighty miles away. It was done.

Chapter Fourteen

Alas, Adventures in Widowerland

> Part of every misery is, so to speak, the misery's shadow or reflection: the fact that you don't merely suffer but have to keep on thinking about the fact that you suffer. I not only live each endless day in grief, but live each day thinking about living each day in grief.
>
> —C. S. Lewis: *A Grief Observed*

Fairly substantially tattooed already I paid a visit one day to Blaby's tattoo studio and had the Japanese symbols for Rhona tattooed on my right hand, something I thought I'd never do. But alongside my life-long love of all things Japanese having these symbols (looking a little like a square above a Christian cross or a letter T) on my right hand meant that I, being right-handed, would see them all the time, especially when writing. I don't regret it for a moment. It's another form of permanent memorial and reminder … or as permanent as anything can be in human life at any rate.

Although technically (albeit in practice or rather non-practice nominally) Jewish, Rhona loved Christmas. She had been raised with some though by no means all of the trappings of Christmas — by now essentially a secular public holiday for most rather than a religious festival for Christians — but in adult life more than made up for it by throwing herself wholeheartedly into the festive season. Christmas, coming hot on the heels of Hanukkah, can be a bit of a tricky area for many secular Jews, perhaps especially those with children raised in a predominantly non-religious culture. Christmas tree or no Christmas tree? Presents for the kids or no presents? Santa or no Santa? And so forth. But for Rhona, Jewish though she undoubtedly was, 'doing' Christmas in style was an absolute given and Christmases at Wareham Road were — at Rhona's direction but predominantly through my sweat and toil — made utterly magical. Earlier in my life I'd had a difficult relationship with the festive season, predominantly on account of the episode of severe-bordering-on-psychotic depression I'd had over the horrific winter of 1991-2, but I had only Rhona to thank for getting me back into the Christmas spirit with a vengeance. Throughout the year I quietly made careful note of the various things that she said she liked, and started buying gifts for her as early as October (or in some cases even the end of September), surreptitiously stowed away in hidey holes until the time came to wrap and tag them. We didn't decorate the entire house but at the earliest possible opportunity (certainly the beginning of December; sometimes even the end of November) the lounge especially — always the beating heart and the soul of our home — was transformed into a Santa's grotto of gaudy Christmas-themed decorations and ornaments, twinkling lights and candles and a six-foot tree weighed down with a ridiculous amount of decorations and at the very least six sets of fairy lights, visible to low Earth orbit let alone passersby. Rhona in her apron would spend hours in the kitchen making a huge batch of her legendarily luscious mince pies; and then there were the hectic shopping expeditions in packed supermarkets. In short, Christmases at Wareham Road were the stuff of absolute magic. There won't be Christmases like that ever again; that's not possible.

Christmas 2018, the first without Rhona, five weeks after her death, was inevitably a very different, almost unendurably bleak affair. For the bereaved, perhaps worst of all for the newly bereaved, significant dates — Christmas; birthdays; anniversaries; any time where celebration, merriment and jollity are expected — are notoriously difficult to negotiate. I expected a dismal time of it and I wasn't wrong. All the same, knowing in advance that I would not see another Christmas at Wareham Road I sought and received permission from Rhona's remaining family to decorate the house this one last time in the manner to which we had been accustomed for nearly the previous two decades. *Of course*, they said. *It's what Rhona would have wanted*. Which in itself was perfectly true (although in *A Grief Observed* C. S. Lewis notes the danger of taking this line of thinking too far: "It's what *X* would have wanted" can very easily slide into "It's what *I* want"). I hung the snowman wreath on the front door; I put up the curtain lights in the dining room; above all else I festooned the lounge with umpteen decorations, umpteen lights, umpteen candles and the always ridiculously over-dressed Christmas tree groaning with half a dozen sets of fairy lights, baubles and tinsel. In the past Christmas had been a convivial, gregarious affair; this time Leah and Claire were spending the holiday with Claire's family and now I had only one person to invite, my elderly aunt Joan, who came over on Christmas Day and Boxing Day both. I had, with almost superhuman effort, been to our local Aldi and back — where Rhona and I had shopped at least two or three times every week for years — to lay in everything necessary for one final, relatively lavish Christmas at what was still my home but would not remain so for very much longer. Rhona-less I was never going to be able to do a Rhona Christmas and wouldn't even have tried, but I did try my level best to do a Christmas that Rhona might have been proud of. I admit that I started drinking early and ended the day colossally drunk and yet — I hope — still managed to acquit myself reasonably honourably and produced a decent Christmas dinner for aunt Joan (I ate next to nothing; at one point I broke down and wept scalding tears over my more or less untouched plate) of which Rhona might have approved. In Christmases past the morning would have been given over to opening presents, in my case book after book after book especially. Now I had just the one present to open, a box from a dear friend containing some cheesy biscuits, a bar of quality dark chocolate and some genuinely appreciated fluffy socks. There was a notable and noticeable absence of Christmas cards; whereas before they had arrived, addressed to Rhona and Steven, in a veritable avalanche, now there were just a few.

I don't remember much else about it. What I do recall (and wish I didn't) is that the festive season, once such a joyous time of year filled with good cheer, wonderful food, lashings of drink and light and colour and warmth and love, was, without Rhona, torturous and would have been worse without keeping myself more or less permanently intoxicated. Days passed in a haze of grief and grief-dulling alcohol. As ever I stayed up to see, on television, 2018 become 2019, listening to Big Ben dole out its dozen bongs before the usual battery of fireworks in central London. Normally Rhona and I would have done this together; as with Christmas Day it would have been one of the very rare occasions when Rhona touched alcohol, typically a (frequently unfinished) small glass of Baileys with lots of ice before going to bed. Now I saw in 2019 without my soulmate. I was alone. *This is life now, Payne. This is how it's going to be. For ever. No Rhona. No more Team Wowo. You're on your own, sunshine.*

Rhona hardly ever touched alcohol, as already noted, but I've always been one for a good drink. On both sides of the family many of the men were hefty boozers and I inherited that gene (or practice, or habit, whatever it may be), so I did what so many desperate and grieving and emotionally crucified people do: I turned to the bottle and hit it hard. In the months that followed Rhona's death I drank heavily. Very heavily indeed, in fact. Well before I had met Rhona I have to admit that I had had relatively brief spells of borderline alcoholism which had always ended when I simply grew bored of the drinking and the hangovers, but now my drinking became very close to frank dipsomania. By preference, a bottle of what's referred to as hard liquor — spirits — a day, not every day but certainly several days a week, wasn't at all unusual, though I drank anything and everything I could lay my hands on; anything to dull the pain, however partially, however temporarily. For the most part I did my shopping online for it to be delivered to the doorstep so I had few and only occasional reasons even to leave the house — mostly for more booze from the nearest shop — so I drank. And drank. And drank. None of this lily-livered wait-until-six-o'-clock nonsense for the Payne; the sun is over the yardarm somewhere in the world all the time, so as soon as I was conscious I got out my favourite glass and started to pour. *Poor me … poor me … pour me another drink.* I'm aware of all the blather about alcoholism and the enormity of the chaos and carnage it causes, not merely to the economy, not merely to the individual, not merely to their families and especially to their children. Don't tell me; I know all this and concede every point. I've heard all the information about heavy drinking and the damage it does; frankly I've heard it all to the point of weariness. As far as we can tell humans have been purposely creating alcoholic beverages since the early Neolithic period, which is to say around 12,000 to 13,000 years ago and they're not going to go anywhere anytime soon. There's a reason for that, or rather several reasons. Chief of those, as far as I'm concerned, is booze's ability to at least temporarily dull emotional pain and to raise spirits and bring a modicum of good if transient cheer. I'm not unsympathetic to anybody in the grip of substance abuse and addiction — quite the antithesis, as a hero of mine, the late, great W. C. Fields was wont to say. All I will say is: in extremis, having been there myself, I will never judge anybody for the methods by which they have to numb themselves enough just to get through one more day. I've been there and done it and cannot, will not sit in judgement on the methods, however harmful and damaging, by which people in an extremity of pain cope with life.

Of course there's scarcely anything surprising about this. In his own memoir of love and loss, *Thinking Out Loud*, the former footballer Rio Ferdinand refers to one study which found that the bereaved make up a quarter of admissions to alcohol rehab centres, while according to another, one in five widowers drink to medically harmful levels. Clearly, when you're not particularly concerned about staying alive, the damage caused by such heavy drinking tends not to be a matter of pressing concern. Why bother, now? The same attitude led me to go back to smoking, albeit in my case pipes and cigars rather than cigarettes; I had once been a twenty-a-day man until I had given up in August 2001 while my mum was dying in hospital. I had developed shortness of breath — clearly stress-related — but I found giving up the cancer sticks trivially easy. I didn't even notice the giving up of nicotine; I had other things on my mind.

The house in Wareham Road — what I had jocularly referred to in my diary as the good ship Wareham with me as the captain whenever Rhona was away — now became Fortress Wareham, locked and curtained against the outside world in self-imposed purdah. Some time before Rhona died I had pissed her off by shaving off my beard — she liked facial hair and preferred me bearded; I merely fancied a change — but now I let the facial furniture grow without trimming. I even let the personal hygiene slide: formerly at least a shower-a-day man, now I simply couldn't be bothered — there didn't seem to be much if any point in washing or in cleaning my teeth — and sat (or laid) in the miasma of my own bodily stink. Unwashed, unshaven and unkempt I sat in my pyjamas and dressing gown in half-light by day behind drawn curtains with the front door locked. Closing the curtains of a house after a death is an old custom now for the most part remembered or practised only by the very old, no doubt for superstitious reasons; I did it to keep the outside world exactly there — outside, where it belonged — and not for a day or two but for months on end. Without a ringing phone and barely any post, two or three days solidly might pass in an alcoholic haze, staring blankly at the TV screen, endlessly watching repeats of favourite programmes from my childhood such as *Minder* and *The Professionals*, passing out in alcohol-induced insensibility for a space only to begin to imbibe again. And so on, round and round and round, as day succeeded to week to month.

Whether through the shattering experience of sheer grief itself, or leaning on alcohol or other drugs legal or illegal or any combination thereof, a great many people — possibly most — find the immediate aftermath of a highly significant loss to be something of a blur. Certainly in the time after Rhona's death while I was still at Wareham Road I relied heavily and variously on Valium to dampen my years-long trait anxiety and cheap spirits to numb, albeit only temporarily, the agonising absence of Rhona — a potentially catastrophic strategy since in combination the two can be dangerous and, in sufficient quantity, possibly even fatal. I never combined the two at the same time — I alternated back and forth between tranquilisers and the cheapest of own-brand liquor — but the grief, the sense of loss, the sheer absence, the utter not-there-ness of Rhona, was so excruciating that to keep myself in a state of numb stupefaction seemed the only course available to me, as so many of the recently bereaved find. Having kept a very regular diary since the age of eleven I was in the habit of taking copious notes about the day's events to be written up at length later on; just as well, since without such notes many of the early days after losing Rhona would be lost altogether. It is also worth noting that Valium can impair the formation of memory, especially I gather short-term memory, so again, without my notes taken on the fly so much of what happened in the earliest days would be gone with the wind.

Although I never took Valium and vodka (or whatever) simultaneously I would be less than fully honest if I didn't say that at various points in the early days, and not especially rarely, thoughts of suicide passed through my mind, something far from unusual amongst the recently bereaved. The desperate, incommunicable crucifixion of grief demanded remedy and while tranquilisers and poor quality Scotch did the trick in the short term — my drinking bordered on the suicidal; at that extent it was certainly a form of self-harm — on occasion a more permanent solution presented itself. There are a hundred and one ways out of life (the hot bath and razor blade; the rope over the rafters; the railway line; the list goes on) but my choice would have been to lapse peacefully and painlessly into an endless (dreamless?) sleep with booze and pills. I certainly had the means at my disposal — I had gallons of spirits in the house and a hefty cache of fatal drugs; in particular my Valium and Rhona's left-over codeine. In *Levels of Life* Julian Barnes writes of his reaction to the death of his wife, the literary agent Pat Kavanagh, in 2008, little more than a month after being diagnosed with a brain tumour:

> The question of suicide arrives early, and quite logically. Most days I pass the stretch of pavement I was looking across at when the idea first came to me. I will give it *x* months, or *x* years (up to a maximum of two), and

> then, if I cannot live without her, if my life is reduced to mere passive continuance, I shall become active. I knew soon enough my preferred method — a hot bath, a glass of wine next to the taps, and an exceptionally sharp Japanese carving knife. I thought of that solution fairly often, and still do. They say (there is a lot of 'they say' around grief and grief-bearing) that thinking about suicide reduces the risk of suicide. I don't know if this is true: for some, it must help them elaborate their planning. So, presumably, thinking about it can cut both ways.

The thought of suicide, Nietzsche famously wrote, is a great consolation; with it one gets through many a bad night. In *Thinking Out Loud* Rio Ferdinand mentions one study which found that 65% of widowers had had what is known in psychiatric circles as 'suicidal ideation' — that is, suicidal thoughts, possibly even plans. Of this percentage a third engaged in self-destructive behaviour such as drinking heavily and taking other drugs; ten per cent had actually made an attempt at ending their own lives. Suicidal thoughts in the face of overwhelming grief are therefore quite common, but for all that it's clearly a grave and desperate state to be in and anybody who finds themselves at such a pass should seek professional help as a matter of dire urgency.

I'm not exaggerating when I say that I believe that had it not been for the presence of our small menagerie I would almost certainly have seen these thoughts through to their conclusion. I'm somewhat shamed to admit to this since my death would have caused colossal pain to my friends and especially to my elderly aunt Joan who was (and remains) my last remaining family member. Be that as it may, as it was I'm convinced that the existence of the dog and the two cats is all that saved me from self-destruction. I had no desire to go on living my own life but I could not and would not abandon the pets to an already overflowing animal shelter goodness only knows where and, worse, an unknown fate in the hands of others. In life Rhona had needed me; now Tilly the dog and

Maxwell and Rosie — the cats — needed me too. I regarded it as a matter of duty that I look after the animals, to tend to their little lives and their concerns just as I had always done when Rhona was still here. A lot of the bereavement stories I've read in the aftermath of Rhona's death have featured children; that's to say people who have — often at a young age — found themselves as widows or widowers but with a child or children, who forced themselves to go on for their sake. As a contentedly childless man my version of a *raison d'etre* was Tilly and the cats. Somehow I lived the words of Samuel Beckett in *The Unnameable*: "You must go on, I can't go on, I'll go on." I'm nobody's idea of a hero and there was no heroism in this; I found not strength but cut-price spirits and prescription medication, and as harmful or even downright dangerous as that is, sometimes it's the only substitute that works — for a time at any rate. It's not good, it's most certainly not healthy and it's nothing I'm proud of, but it's a fact all the same. Julian Barnes found his own way through his suicidal phase:

> I realised that, insofar as she was alive at all, she was alive in my memory. Of course, she remained powerfully in other people's minds as well; but I was her principal rememberer. If she was anywhere, she was within me, internalised [...] I could not kill myself because then I would also be killing her. She would die a second time, my lustrous memories of her fading as the bathwater turned red.

Brood on suicide I may have done, but the thoughts that I most quickly quelled and would not allow myself to think were those about the desire to have died instead of Rhona in order to have evaded the torment I was in. As understandable as this may be — at least to some —, every time it arose in my mind I instantly quashed it, scolding myself for my rank selfishness. Rhona was ill and getting weaker; at various points she needed constant care and pretty well everything doing for her. If I had died on November 17th 2018 (or at any other point after her kidneys failed come to that) she would have been left high and dry, utterly stranded and dependent upon piecemeal care from goodness only knows what sources. Pain may make us self-absorbed but thoughts of this kind demonstrated a nadir of selfishness I wouldn't allow myself to stoop to.

Daylight hours were for the most part just about minimally tolerable. A lot of the time I drank all day — just alcohol, no food — or, when (rarely) not drinking, busied body and to a certain extent distracted the mind in strenuous housework. Both in Stevenage and in Blaby I had always been a conscientious house husband while Rhona was alive; I saw no reason to change now that she wasn't. Keeping the house, our home, our nest, ship-shape remained important to me even though there was no Rhona to do it for and no Rhona to see the results of my labours. A ragged, shaggy, smelly, disorganised and disorderly mess I may have been on the personal level but I retained some semblance of self-respect at least to that extent. This is still — not for long, but still — my home; I like a nice neat, clean and tidy home; therefore I keep it spick and span. It's what I do. Being physically active and having something to concentrate upon helped to a degree. Unfortunately I quickly found that while one can flick around a duster at any time of the day or night one can't maniacally vacuum the carpets at three o'clock in the morning because you're monumentally pissed and have taken it into your drink-addled head to do so; in the latter case the neighbours tend not to approve.

Eventually night would fall, early at that time of year. All my life I've been in a minority in being a confirmed lover of winter; its early but fiery sunsets; its crisp but blazing frosty mornings and rare snows; the snugness of premature nightfall and drawing curtains and lighting lights against the darkness, the primal, primeval, atavistic cosiness of the den, sett and burrow. There aren't many of us around but we do exist; we're like a secret society. But now winter took on its most terrible aspect. As the day began to wind down I knew with a sinking dread that the long winter hours of darkness were beginning and the far deeper, infinitely blacker blackness of grief, loss and absence was about to kick in. In bed or (frequently and increasingly) on the couch, massively drunk or sober (far more often the former), asleep, awake or somewhere in between, I cried aloud for Rhona, loud enough I'm sure for even the neighbours to have heard me through brick walls.

Rhona.

Rhona.

Rhona.

Where are you?

Why did you leave me?

Rhona?

Rhona!

Rhona?

No answer.

In Tennyson's great monument to grief at the death of his friend Arthur Henry Hallam, *In Memoriam* — perhaps the greatest poem of bereavement ever written — he speaks of there being no language but a cry. Sometimes, in extremis, a cry is all we have and all we can do. I cried aloud in the darkest reaches of the night and received no response. A cry was uttered but of course answer came there none. The silence, the absence, was absolute.

Chapter Fifteen

Solo

> I would always look for clues to her in books and poems, I realized. I would always search for the echoes of the lost person, the scraps of words and breath, the silken ties that say, Look: she existed.
>
> —Meghan O'Rourke

I'm an only child and have always been an essentially solitary man, and until I met Rhona I'd always relished a healthy proportion of solitude; Anthony Storr's lovely and fascinating book of that name has been a lifelong favourite. I have only ever had a small circle of very close friends. As a confirmed introvert I've always enjoyed my own company; once upon a time I was my own best friend. But now, especially at night but also at random times during the day, not merely the simple state of being agreeably alone — the quiet balm of solitude — but true loneliness bit and bit hard; brutally, savagely hard. Sometimes, as Alphonse de Lamartine famously put it, one person is missing and the whole world seems depopulated, a sentiment echoed almost word for word in our own time by Joan Didion: "A single person is missing for you and the whole world is empty." When my mum had taken ill in 2001 and died so suddenly from peritonitis Rhona had been my support. (Come to that she had been my support in everything). Now, with Rhona gone, my support had vanished. I moved like a wraith through an empty, semi-dark house, frequently colossally drunk, noting in appalling agony this and that thing from the life that Rhona and I had shared for so long. The cheap chiming clock on the wall inherited years before from my parents which annoyed Zena on her rare visits to our home but which we got used to and grew almost to love. Our best, sharpest bread knife with the black handle in the cutlery drawer. The radio on the kitchen windowsill — a Christmas present from a few years earlier — on which Rhona listened to her beloved LBC while she was cooking or making sandwiches to take to dialysis. Her favourite glass coffee mugs. The household minutiae of every and any couple; the stuff of everyday life; our life.

People — Rhona's friends; my friends; common friends; our near neighbours — were uniformly immensely kind. I was fortunate to escape the sometimes cruel but more often wholly well-intentioned but thoughtless, awkward and embarrassed reactions that so many of the recently bereaved can describe; the avoidance-in-the-street syndrome to which multitudes of the bereft can attest only too well. So many people are embarrassed by grief in others — perhaps afraid that they will say the wrong thing; perhaps disturbed by a reminder of their own mortality — as C. S. Lewis notes in *A Grief Observed*:

> I'm aware of being an embarrassment to everyone I meet. At work, at the club, in the street, I see people, as they approach me, trying to make up their minds whether they'll 'say something about it' or not. I hate it if they do, and if they don't. Some funk it altogether. R. has been avoiding me for a week.

The house was filled with cards of sympathy and condolence, many containing heartfelt messages of love and sorrow for Rhona and gratitude that I cared for her in her final illness. Surprisingly and touchingly there were even cards from Rhona's private dental practice and the staff of the ITU at Leicester General hospital, neither of which I had ever expected and by which I was greatly moved. Bunches of flowers were brought to the door; offers of help extended and, though not taken up, were much and genuinely appreciated. Thank-you letters and emails were written and sent. Still; many, I would say most bereaved people find that even in the closest and most loving of their relatives and friends something akin to bereavement fatigue eventually sets in and sooner or later one is left to one's own devices. There is usually no conscious cruelty or callousness in this; after all people have their own families, their own affairs, their own troubles and concerns that have to be attended to. People trot out the line 'life goes on' but they mean that it goes on *for them.* It simply means that people have to go back to their own lives — get the kids to school; take the car in for its MoT; book that appointment at the dentist; push a trolley around Morrisons; the stuff of everyday life — while the mourner attends to the business of their grief alone. It can scarcely be any other way.

I did a great deal of housework and a very great deal of drinking. One thing of which I did almost none was cry. Not because the impulse was not there — quite the contrary — but because I quite deliberately prevented myself from doing so. The self-destructive impulse was at the root of this too. A couple of weeks after Rhona's death I jotted down in my notebook:

> I am deliberately, consciously and explicitly preventing myself from crying; whenever the tears rise and the lump forms in my throat I swallow it back down, prey as I am to the perhaps superstitious, perhaps utterly unfounded and fallacious, possible old wives' tale that unexpressed grief causes mental and possibly even physical harm. This may be long since discredited quasi-Freudian claptrap, but I do it all the same.

I have no idea whether the modern medical world still sets any store in the old belief that buried, even deliberately suppressed grief causes somatic illness or whether such thinking has gone the way of the four humours and leeches. I'd be very interested to know. Nevertheless, as I've said, the urge to do myself harm was at the root of it and whenever

I felt tears begin to prick my eyes and that only too familiar lump in the throat began to form I shook myself and carried on with something else to distract me from giving into a torrential river of tears that just might never stop.

Anybody who has ever lost anybody so very close and dear to them will know that the most seemingly small, trivial, insignificant things take on an importance, a specialness, out of all proportion to what might seem to be their worth to outsiders. Various people had warned me not to become too attached to things, but every facet and every artefact of the life that Rhona and I had shared so closely for so long became charged with significance; her favourite white mug, the fact that we shopped at the local Aldi and Waitrose every few days every week, her innumerable scarves (*Why does one person need so* many?) hanging in the cloakroom, trips to the post office practically every other day with multiple eBay parcels, a million and one things. As bizarre as it may sound to anybody but the bereaved, one of the most heart-rending tasks that had to be carried out in the weeks and months after Rhona's death was getting rid of food in the cupboards, fridges and freezers which I knew we had bought together or in some cases food which Rhona had herself actually made. For those in grief it may be more common than we realise; there's a good reason why Michel Faber, in *Undying*, the collection of poems written about, for and to his late wife Eva, included two poems ('Risotto' and 'Tamarind') about exactly this phenomenon.

It had to be disposed of in one way or another because I certainly wasn't prepared to enjoy any of it. Although I'd eaten relatively well at the post-funeral gathering, now my appetite as good as disappeared and I began to lose weight — a lot of weight — very rapidly, leading to kindly-meant but pointed observations from those around me on my increasing gauntness. Eating next to nothing I was left alone in a silent house with our customarily full cupboards, fridges and freezers. Rhona was an avid shopper (and before she became ill a big eater) and insisted on both large fridge-freezers (one in the kitchen, the other in the garage) and the kitchen cupboards being stuffed to capacity at all times. Now it all languished as a memento of the love and the life I'd lost. Tins, packets and bottles with best before or use-by dates on them were a personal and outrageous affront; not merely atrociously painful but actively offensive. What good is a tin of something that says 'use by September 2019' or a jar of herbs marked 'best before April 2020' when my soulmate and the love of my life is dead and buried? Even food in the two fridges, left untouched for long enough, began to spoil and had to be thrown away including — perhaps worst of all, with the exception of food that Rhona had herself made — some of her favourite foods left half-eaten when Rhona was so suddenly snatched away. On the same day that Rhona died I dug out from my desk a small, until then unused black notebook I had bought not long beforehand and started to write down whatever stray thoughts that passed through my numb and addled mind such as the one given above; a journal of grief, a companion to my much more detailed diary rather in the manner of C. S. Lewis's *A Grief Observed.* On the day after Rhona's death I jotted down:

> There is a half-eaten rice pudding and a half-eaten dish of jelly in the kitchen fridge at this very moment. *Fieri sentio et excrucior* [Catullus: I feel it happening and am in agony].

These had been left in the fridge on the Tuesday that Rhona went off to dialysis and never came back to her home again. Rhona had recently been having extensive (and because private, expensive) dental treatment — which as a severe dental-phobic she feared and hated with passionate dread and relied on Valium to get her through the ordeal — and had latterly been living largely on mush. Rice pudding and jelly; sludge; baby food; half-eaten, put back in the fridge to be finished on some other day, a day that never came. Half-finished rice pudding and jelly in bowls in a fridge in a kitchen in a house; the most painful things in the world.

Although a practical measure, knowing, remembering that we had been in precisely this or that shop or supermarket when this food was bought and now had to be discarded, the agony of this cannot be described. These items became my secular equivalent of Catholic holy relics, like supposed fragments of the true cross or the bones of this or that saint. The house became a three-bedroomed semi-detached reliquary. These days the word *fetish* is used and heard almost exclusively in a sexual sense (whips and chains and leather boots in dungeons and what have you) but originally it's a term from anthropology used of certain objects in indigenous cultures — West African tribes; native American Indians — believed to possess a mysterious supernatural force which has power over people. In that sense the relics, to mix my religious metaphors, were fetishes. This tin of soup or that packet of noodles was something that Rhona had chosen; something she had looked at, pored over, bought, be it in Aldi, Waitrose, Tesco, Sainsbury's, Asda, Morrison's (all local to us. We always were not just very regular but promiscuous shoppers, never loyal to one specific supermarket); something that Rhona had once — not merely once but recently — physically and actually *touched*. I very slowly worked my way over a period of several months through the frozen foods, mostly vegetables but including (even though I have been a vegetarian almost all my adult life) a tray of frozen salmon fishcakes lovingly, painstakingly made by Rhona shortly before her death which I felt I ought to eat rather than throw away. I am still a confirmed vegetarian bordering on vegan and expect to remain so but I have to say that they were, as per Rhona's usual standard, utterly delicious. Tinned, jarred and packet goods with a long shelf life were bagged up and donated to a foodbank, hopefully to do some good to the needy. Otherwise I had the appetite of an anorexic mouse and despite my frankly colossal intake of alcohol — even though booze is merely empty calories, we're told; the best kind in my view — I continued to lose weight for many more months. Over time one stone disappeared; then another; then another; then another; then another. I was dwindling, as Rhona had done as illness took hold. Not that I had any appetite for food in any case but doubtless there was an element of deliberate self-harm in this too; a form of anorexia nervosa perhaps, perhaps even a slow, camouflaged suicide. Maybe I was trying to disappear, to evaporate, to absent myself from the world by degrees.

Rhona's favourite programmes on the Sky+ box — on series link and still being recorded daily and weekly — were another source of indescribable anguish. I didn't watch them (they were, with some notable exceptions, Rhona's thing and I hadn't been interested in many of them even when she was alive. I never did see the appeal of *Masterchef* and *Strictly Come Dancing*, myself) but I couldn't bring myself to delete them and so allowed them to accumulate. The very idea of deleting them cut too close to the psychic bone of deleting Rhona and the things she had still enjoyed in the late, limited final weeks and days of her life. A pair of black trousers left hanging on the hook on the bathroom door on the final day that she went off to dialysis was another fount of agony. Rhona's laundry, still in the washing basket on the landing from her last day and awaiting the attention of the washing machine and iron, yet another. The smallest things such as these, perhaps precisely because they're the smallest things and therefore easier to process than the enormous fact of death, were the most unspeakably painful and caused transports of atrocious agony. For all that, like Miss Havisham I wanted to keep the house exactly as it was on the day that Rhona had left it as far as possible, static, frozen like a time capsule, a danger sign of complicated grief according to Meghan O'Rourke; aside from having to throw out spoilt food (which I found inordinately painful) almost the only thing I allowed myself to change was to unplug the telephone in the bedroom since it contained — it still contains, as far as I'm aware, which is why just like Jonathan Santlofer in *The Widower's Notebook* I've kept it — Rhona's recorded answerphone message, Rhona's *voice*, Rhona herself, a healthy Rhona, a living Rhona, a Rhona who had had several attempts at recording a message until she got to the one she was satisfied with. *Hello, can't get to the phone right now; please leave a message and we'll get back to you.* Then the usual electronic squeal. Phone calls were few and far between but this was too much to bear. I unplugged the phone and put it and its base unit away.

As co-executor of Rhona's will Leah took over and did the lion's share of the spade-work inevitable following any death, though I cancelled this direct debit and that standing order and this membership of such-and-such. Despite this, from time to time post still arrived addressed to MRS RHONA SHAFIK or occasionally MRS RHONA PAYNE since for a few non-essential purposes Rhona sometimes used my surname. Another stab in the heart.

These moments had a distinct and discrete cause, an obvious trigger, but there cannot be a single bereaved person on the face of the planet unfamiliar with the utterly random piercing attacks (I use the word attack deliberately) of overwhelming, unbearable grief and shattering loneliness that strike indiscriminately at any hour of the day or night; lacerating assaults of intolerable sorrow that lie in wait like some ferocious wild beast only to pounce at the most seemingly trivial moments — washing a mug at the sink; sitting on the toilet; blankly turning the pages of a book or newspaper; pushing a trolley around a supermarket; trying to concentrate on a TV programme; standing in a queue in the post office waiting to send a letter or a parcel; anytime, anywhere. In *The Presence*, the journal kept by the Welsh doctor and poet Dannie Abse in the wake of the 2005 death of his wife Joan in a road accident he wrote:

> I may be sitting in an armchair reasonably undisturbed, embedded in unstressful idleness, thinking about this or that, about inconsequential matters, or reading a book or listening to music or watching TV when suddenly I realise that Joan isn't upstairs in her study, nor in the kitchen preparing a meal, nor outside working in the garden, nor shopping, nor visiting an art gallery, and then I feel again the disquiet of her absences which makes me involuntarily cry out 'Oh Joan!' I try to dam the impetuous gush of tears. And I think less than a year ago she did this, she did that, it's not possible, it is not true. But then I know it is true …

It *is* true. It can't be true. *But it is. She's gone.* Not only a year but weeks ago Rhona was here, right here, there, doing this, doing that. Now she is — perhaps — nobody and nowhere save in my memory of her being here and there doing this and doing that. Perhaps.

My mind returned to what seemed like an apt passage in a favourite novel I'd read years earlier: A. N. Wilson's 1993 novel *The Vicar of Sorrows*. Simply put, the Reverend Francis Kreer is a middle-aged, conventional Church of England vicar who in short order faces a twin loss: the death of his elderly mother and the loss of his faith in God. (There's far, far more to the plot than that, of course, but these two events are the driving force behind much of what occurs). Francis is unmanned by the depth of his grief at losing his mother; for the first time in his life he is truly confronted with the agony of loss, not vicariously (pun unintentional) in others but in himself:

> Pain now came upon him, great stabs of it. He could never have predicted how horrified, and surprised, he would be by his mother's death; and the pain which it now occasioned was, he realised, only the beginning of a long cycle of agony. Phrases such as the indifference of the fates, the cruelty of the universe, which had earlier been to him no more than words, now matched his mood entirely [...] The world went on being cruelly the same, even though, each day, some death caused another human being pain such as he suffered now. The densely-populated London scene which stretched around him outside the window suddenly seemed like a laboratory full of squealing animals in which mad scientists were practising their tortures on rats and mice. There was not a home or block of flats in view which had not once contained someone feeling as he felt now: raw and vulnerable and searingly sad. In every dwelling, there was someone who was compelled to confront their own mortality, perhaps a painful death by cancer or a debilitating old age. And when the horrible process had been consummated and the journey to the crematorium had been made, there would be this, for someone left behind: this scalding pain, this terrible pain which could not be controlled, and which was worse than anyone had ever warned him!

> He had 'counselled' many bereaved people himself. He had watched their eyes fill and refill with tears every time they tried to stammer out their feelings. He had seen the pain, but he had never appreciated how bad it could be [...] He felt weak with the pain and anguish which this death had caused. He felt as though great holes had been gouged in his head, his body; as though some fiend had hacked a hole in the back of his head, and another in his breast, and as though a cold wind were blowing through his body. He felt cold. And so very, very tired. And exposed. Still, he continued to stare at the indifferent sky and the heartless trees which blew gently in the gathering darkness. And this, he thought, is the universe which they tell us was created by and for Love!

For the first three months or so after Rhona's death until David and Leah arrived to begin the process of clearing the house I existed (I almost wrote *lived* but in reality it was bare existence) alone. I sat, drank and slept surrounded by Rhona's things — *our* things, the stuff of our everyday life together for more than two decades. Subsequently several friends opined that this may not have been such a good idea; that I was rubbing salt into the wound by remaining in the home we had created and shared for eighteen years and that I should have moved out to somewhere else, anywhere else, at the earliest opportunity. It's a point of view but not one that, on the whole, I share. Did I do the right thing in staying on for as long as I did? I believe so, as painful as it was to sleep in our king-sized bed and to fall asleep each night listening to LBC as Rhona had done for so long, the empty other side of the bed a perpetual reminder of loss. Yet it was something that I felt I had to do. As I've mentioned before I was solemnly advised to hold onto memories and not to get too attached to mere things. I can, at a push, understand the rationale behind such advice but these were not mere things to me but the stuff of our life together, day in and day out. I'm not materialistic and don't believe for a moment that I'm unduly motivated by the acquisition of 'stuff' for its own sake, but the household things by which I was surrounded were the objects of our everyday life. As with food, even the best and sharpest bread knife in the cutlery drawer,

Rhona's favourite mug, the pots and pans, the utensils, the spice racks, the ornaments and knick-knacks, the cheap clock on the mantelpiece, Rhona's numerous cookbooks; these things — everything, in fact — became imbued with import, with meaning and significance as emblems of a life shared for so very long and which was now no longer shared and never could be shared again. They were — they *are* — imbued not with monetary value but with what is for me the greatest value of all, namely sentimental value. They were — they *are* — imbued with something that I can only call Rhona-ness, the state or quality of having been seen by Rhona, wanted by Rhona, chosen by Rhona, frequently bought by Rhona, handled by Rhona, liked by Rhona.

Physically, mentally, psychologically, emotionally, whatever you want to call it, I was in freefall. I had had some unspeakably awful experiences in my life to that point, most notably the first and easily the worst skirmish with extremely severe depression in the winter of 1991-1992 when I was nineteen — worse even, more excruciating I am ashamed to have to say, than the death of my mum a decade later — but these months in the immediate aftermath of Rhona's death, although I wanted and doubtless needed the solitude, were without any question whatever the blackest, bleakest and most desperate period of my lifetime. There is always something a little bit too auto-back-slapping, too self-congratulatory, too how-noble-am-I about these comments for my taste, but frankly I don't know how I survived these months. There was Tilly and there were the cats, of course, but I would say long stretches of unconsciousness, mindless telly and borderline suicidal levels of alcohol intake, on the whole. Whatever else, in the absence of any kind of religious or spiritual belief/support system … I don't know. Survival at times became a matter of merely clinging on, not even from day to day but from one hour to the next.

Many bereaved people say that, at some point or other, they somehow feel the distinct presence of the loved one they have lost; a sense that they, though physically absent, are in some indefinable way still *there*. In grief auditory and even visual hallucinations (if indeed that is what they are) — thinking that you've heard the lost loved one's voice or that you've caught sight of them in a crowd of people — are surprisingly common. I envy such people immensely as I never did and never have had such a sensation. Not yet at any rate. I have longed desperately for some crumb of the assurance that some bereaved people experience, the heartfelt certainty that their loved and lost one is still around in some form, but for me there was and has only ever been the gaping, glaring, heart-tearing no-longer-there-ness of the love of my life and soulmate. As Barbara Want writes in *Why Not Me?*:

> … I began to understand for the first time why no one ever tells you about the torment that is grief. It is greater than you can know. It takes you to a terrifying place located at the outer edges of human tolerance. And at its furthest and most frightening point it plays one last card as it reminds you — with seeming glee — that the one person who always rescued you from the brink, who was always there for you at the worst of times and whom you now need more than ever, is not there, is not anywhere, and never will be again. The breast that you would lean on, the arms that would embrace you, are not there. In their place is a howling void.

Dannie Abse called his journal of the first year of bereavement *The Presence*: for me there has only ever been absence, hence the title of this part of the book. Rhona was technically Jewish but non-religious. So am I. I cannot, hand on heart, honestly say that I believe, fully and truly and honestly believe, that there is some essential spark, some element of the individual person which persists after death. I had previously never understood those non-believers who spoke enviously of religious belief but I understand it now. I wish that I did and could share such beliefs; I positively want it to be the case because in that situation there is a chance that I will meet Rhona again, added to which it — *I* — might be emotionally healthier if I could seriously take such a thing as being true. But I'm too mindful of Iris Murdoch's bleak but as far as I can see accurate dictum that whatever consoles us is fake. Over and over and over I find myself caught in the same old web. I don't believe. I want to believe. I don't believe. I want to believe. I don't believe. I *want* to believe. But I can no more make myself believe something which I don't actually think is true any more than I can make myself fly. As someone, I can't recall who, once put it, I can no more believe the (to me) unbelievable than I can say the unsayable.

Though I existed alone at this period I wasn't entirely without contact with the outside world after a fashion. I got in touch with various bereavement support organisations including the estimable Cruse, though I was surprised to be told gently that it was too soon for them to offer me any support; needing to process my grief in my own way and at my own time I was asked to contact them at a later date — several months hence — if I felt that I still needed their help. I joined Widowed and Young, an organisation for those under the age of fifty who have lost a spouse or partner. At forty-six I hadn't considered myself to be still young but fifty is the cut-off point and I just qualified. I've never been entirely sure about the alleged benefits of counselling or therapy but later on I saw a succession of bereavement counsellors (something that apparently widows are twice as likely to do as widowers) until, after a couple of false starts, I finally settled on N., a friendly, sympathetic and approachable young woman who came to the house weekly (this time I had to open the curtains if only for an hour) to let me pour out my grief and — finally — weep plentiful and scalding tears, which I found surprisingly easy to do in front of a complete stranger. It would be hard for me to put into words what good this did, has done me; as an introvert and in many respects an admittedly closed person I've never been convinced of the benefits of talking things over with others (something of which Rhona was well aware and of which she was critical) but perhaps simply having a neutral but kindly observer to talk to about Rhona and how her loss had devastated me was enough in and of itself. Clearly I must have got something or other from it since I've kept it up for many months — at time of writing, almost ten months after Rhona's death, I'm keeping it up still. Perhaps the first anniversary will be the appropriate time to terminate the arrangement. I don't know. Prior to Rhona's death I would never have imagined myself saying this (but prior to Rhona's death I was in some respects a different man) but now

I would actively recommend that the bereaved look into, or at the very least consider, some form of bereavement counselling. Nothing suits all cases and I concede that it may not necessarily be for everybody, but I would never have thought that it would help me and yet it has been invaluable. There's nothing to be lost by giving it a try save a modest investment in time and an initially small amount of money. I can only reiterate (slightly) the words of Jonathan Santlofer: "I am no longer a man who cannot cry. I am a man who cannot stop crying."

Rhona was and is the companion and presence in my life and will ever be so; but as Donald Hall once said of Jane Kenyon, after November 17th 2018 my companion was and is her absence. I can't imagine that there will ever not be a time when I unthinkingly, forgetfully turn to one side or to the other to share something just heard — a joke, a snippet of news or an item of current affairs, an observation, a quote, a comment — and find only nothingness at my side. As far as I am concerned there can be no getting over that.

Chapter Sixteen

A Hole in the World

> Where you used to be, there is a hole in the world, which I find myself constantly walking around in the daytime, and falling in at night.
>
> —Edna St. Vincent Millay

After bereavement almost all people find that their powers of concentration are shot and even avid readers, as I have been for much of my life, are barely capable of sustaining attention from one paragraph to the next let alone from page to page. We're all familiar with the experience of reading while tired and having to go back to re-read a passage which simply didn't sink in; for the grieving that becomes the default state. For many months after Rhona's death I read nothing (and moreover *wanted* to read nothing) but poetry; specifically the poetry of mourning, grief and bereavement — Donald Hall's *Without* and *The Painted Bed*, Michel Faber's *Undying*, Christopher Reid's *A Scattering* and Douglas Dunn's *Elegies*, all collections of heart-rending poetry about the illnesses (cancer in each case here) and deaths of beloved wives, were constantly at my side. A full-length book was utterly beyond me and would remain so for months; but with the attention span of a gnat with learning difficulties, poetry — short and sharp and to the point — was still doable. "Poetry," wrote Donald Hall, "gives the griever not release from grief but companionship in grief." I had written verse myself in the past (I've never been confident enough to dignify my output with the honourable title of poetry) and in my desolation I suddenly found an efflorescence of inspiration; I began to write verses about (for? to?) Rhona too which eventually became a slender volume called *Paperwork*, at time of writing published just a month ago. Later, idly leafed through and picked over like an unwanted meal, there were the non-fiction books about the same dismal subjects; there were advisory books on bereavement, manuals on how to 'do' grief as healthily as possible, some excellent, some useless and many somewhere in between. And then there were the misery memoirs by the bereaved — Donald Hall's *The Best Day, The Worst Day*; Barbara Want's *Why Not Me?;* Joyce Carol Oates's *A Widow's Story*; Lucie Brownlee's *Life After You*; Joan Didion's *The Year of Magical Thinking*; Maddy Paxman's *The Great Below*; Geoff Mead's *Gone in the Morning*; plenty of others. In some cases I read those death-haunted books penned in advance by the still living but terminally ill; Ivan Noble, Oliver Sacks, Jenny Diski, Nina Riggs. This too was an element of the grieving process: we read, as C. S. Lewis famously said, to know that we are not alone (personally I would add that writing fulfils the same function). I'm not convinced by this; in my experience sooner or later fundamentally everyone who grieves grieves alone. But given the unbearable loneliness that follows loss, to read about the experiences of bereavement of others can be upsetting in the extreme but can also offer certain morbid, curious but undeniable comforts of its own. Perhaps these books and all the others I have read but not mentioned were exercises in teaching me to try to write about bereavement as I have tried to do here. Since, as Geoff Mead puts it, grief is *terra incognita* to us until it actually happens, those who have ventured into its dark and gruesome woods are more likely to seek out roadmaps by those who have travelled that loneliest and grimmest of paths before us. This phenomenon, while not necessarily universal, seems to be incredibly common. As Lucie Brownlee writes in *Life After You*, referring to the immediate aftermath of the sudden death of her young husband Mark:

> I trawled the Internet for books on grief and underwent an ordering frenzy that resulted in a pile of bereavement literature being delivered to my door. I read voraciously. How had other people got through this? What was the answer to this devastating conundrum?

And Meghan O'Rourke, in *The Long Goodbye*:

> I sit here in my tiny study, bills dropped on the floor, books piling by the desk—*Death and Western Thought*, *Death's Door*, *The Denial of Death*, *This Republic of Suffering*—believing in some primitive part of my brain that if I read them all, if I learn everything there is to know, I'll solve the problem. I will find the answer to the equation.

The relentless search for answers … Perhaps surprisingly I read very little of the technical literature on grief and bereavement; as interesting and useful as they may undoubtedly be to professionals in the field I preferred human accounts by real people rather than dry scientific analyses by specialists.

The poetry and prose of loss, like that of love (ignoring for the moment the obvious overlap between the two), is some of the finest there is and is an almost equally large field. One poem amongst many which spoke to me in particular is well-known; 'The Exequy' by Henry King, Bishop of Chichester (1592-1669) on the premature death of his wife Anne in 1624. Not all of the specifics mirrored my own situation; they were relatively closely matched in age, they had several children (of which only two survived past infancy) and Anne died at the age of only twenty-four, for example ("Thou scarce hadst seen so many years/ As day tells hours") and within a couple of years King had remarried. Nevertheless it is a remarkable monument to a lost wife and the only poem by which King is now remembered (especially the most famous segment of the long elegy, the dozen lines beginning "Sleep on, my Love, in thy cold bed"), exploring, explaining and simply exhibiting his desolation and his fervent Christian assurance that he and Anne would be reunited after death. It is not remotely coincidental that Dannie Abse chose to include the poem as an appendix to his book *The Presence* and I have followed suit.

Grief makes philosophers of us all, after a fashion. It could be that all bereaved people experience a crisis of meaning in the wake of a shattering loss, an existential crisis about the purpose of their lives, about where they fit in the world and not merely what they are to do but what they are to *be* after their loss. In *The Long Goodbye*, her memoir about the death of her mother and its aftermath, Meghan O' Rourke writes: "When you lose someone you were close to, you have to reassess your picture of the world and your place in it. The more your identity is wrapped up with the deceased, the more difficult the mental work." I suspect this is particularly true of the remaining half of a couple and even more so if the survivor had been a carer. I think it's important for both halves of a couple to have their own interests and to have their own pursuits lest one half becomes a mere mirror, a cipher; but all the same, to be one half of a couple is to a large extent to have oneself defined as a reflection of the other. For very close to twenty-one years I was one half of Team Wowo; not so much Steven as "...andSteven", as in RhonaandSteven, as though we were one indivisible, inseparable unit neither one of which really works without the other, the equivalent of "... and chips" or "... and Wise" or "... and Hardy". Which I believe we were. For the last three and a half of those years I of course adopted another, newer role, that of Rhona's carer — as I've outlined there were lengthy stretches, especially at the beginning of her renal failure before haemodialysis started to make a difference, where she was couch-bound, unable to go further than the downstairs lavatory (and even then with a walking frame) and required full care pretty much around the clock, needing to be washed, dressed, undressed, dressed and fed on the special renal failure diet.

All of these roles abruptly fell away as soon as Rhona died. I was ... well, what exactly *was* I? I was no longer half of a partnership, no longer fifty per cent of the union of two lovers in their lover's story, no longer in what was a marriage in all but the formal, legal sense. I was no longer "... andSteven" because there was no Rhona to make up RhonaandSteven. As Barbara Want puts it in *Why Not Me?*: "I wasn't even half of the couple we had been: I was but a fraction." I was no longer a carer. I was no longer the man willing to give up one of his own kidneys to save Rhona's life; not because I had become unwilling but because it was now superfluous. I had been Rhona's partner, lover, best friend, house husband and then, at the end, her carer as well. She was, in every sense of these superficially glib but to me entirely meaningful phrases, the love of my life and my soulmate, someone with whom I was perfectly in tune and on the same wavelength. I had, in general ways but especially in the case of being a carer for someone chronically ill, been needed. I had had things to do — important, perhaps even vital things. I had shown up. I had been useful. What, then, was I now? What was my role? What do I do with my life? What am I *for? Without Rhona, what was I?* I'm still, even now, trying to find answers to those questions. Perhaps there are no answers to be had. Or perhaps there is just one: I used to think *I write therefore I am* but now that there is no better reason to write than about Rhona, whether in prose or in what I laughingly call verse, that has been revised to *Rhona was, and I write about Rhona, therefore since Rhona was, I am.*

Then again, maybe the only role by which I could now identify myself was as The Widower. Not *the widower*, or even *a widower*, but The Widower, like a stock character in a play. Not that Rhona and I were ever formally or legally married — I wish we had been — but in all the relevant senses our relationship was a marriage; a union of bodies to begin with and then hearts, minds. Souls, some might say. We went almost everywhere together, did most things together, shared everything; exactly what is a marriage if not that? Now that Rhona was gone I could no longer call myself The Partner, The House Husband, The Carer so I had to be The Widower, with all that that entails.

So much has been written about the so-called stages model of grief — typically listed as denial; anger; bargaining; depression; acceptance — popularised by the Swiss-American psychiatrist Elisabeth Kübler-Ross in her seminal 1969 book *On Death and Dying*. Unfortunately such a great deal of what has been written about the Kübler-Ross model is as far as I'm concerned arrant nonsense. Critics (of whom there are many; justifiably in my view) point out firstly that it lacks empirical support. For another thing Kübler-Ross's work was about the alleged stages of grief she had observed *in the terminally ill* — those who were themselves dying, not those who had been bereaved. Somewhere along the line the stages of grief model crossed over from being about the dying to being about the bereaved and Kübler-Ross later expressed some regret at the lack of clarity with which she had presented her model; she had never intended to suggest that it was linear and that all of the bereaved move through each stage sequentially. On the whole it would seem to be an idea which has had its day. In *The Essential Guide to Grief and Grieving* Debra Holland writes:

> The problem with using Elisabeth Kübler-Ross's original stages model is that it takes the myriad reactions that comprise grief and forces them into five boxes. The stages work well for people who are dying, but they don't always fit those grieving a death or other losses. While some people may find themselves grieving in the five stages, most people don't.

Grief, especially the grief of bereavement, doesn't unfold in orderly stages. Some people might not pass through any of the stages. The reality is that grief is individual and fluid. Painful emotions may come in waves, they may "pop up" unexpectedly during times of feeling "normal", or a certain emotion may be continuously present before subsiding.

If people try to squeeze themselves into the five-stages model, they may find they don't fit. They may feel something is wrong with them if they don't. Or others can try to force the bereaved into a certain stage and criticize them if they show a different reaction. The stages don't take into account that someone's passing, while sad, can also be a loving and spiritual experience.

In my experience at any rate there are no 'stages' of grief; only cycling tsunamis of horrendous heartache that lie in wait only to pounce from the undergrowth without warning and without notice.

That said, for myself denial or disbelief were paramount; the sheer inability truly to grasp the fact of Rhona's not-there-ness. I didn't experience bargaining (with whom? God doesn't apply) nor did I experience any anger as there was no one and nothing to be angry with or about, and in any case anger would have been one of the most sublimely pointless, useless reactions however natural it may be for some in different circumstances. I'm certainly not saying that there have never been situations in life where I haven't lost my rag, gone ape, blown my stack and completely lost my shit but generally speaking I'm a pretty placid man with a very long fuse. I can do irked annoyance and irritation as well as the next man as long as the next man is Victor Meldrew but I don't really 'do' anger, or at least certainly not very often or for very long. With whom or what would I have been angry? God? I'm not religious, and although I try to be respectful of sincerely held beliefs I am puzzled by those who are and have to square the circle of believing in a presumably loving God who nevertheless takes away (or at least allows to be taken) the ones we love and cherish most in the world. I can't be brought to believe in a good, loving, benevolent God who presumably created death in its plan for creation and the hideous pain that accompanies it. (There is the, to me, specious and sophistical response of those like Rabbi Harold Kushner in his worldwide best-seller *When Bad Things Happen to Good People* that the God in which he believes is all-good but not all-powerful — a benevolent but limited God who *wants* to end suffering but cannot. I am as constitutionally incapable of these mental gymnastics as I am of the physical variety). Hospital staff? They couldn't have cared for Rhona any better or with gentler, more tender and solicitous care than they did. Myself? Closer, possibly, but I was more disappointed in myself that I couldn't donate a kidney. Disappointed, not angry. Rhona, for leaving me? This is very far from unknown — Joyce Carol Oates in *A Widow's Story* writes eloquently of her anger at her husband Raymond Smith for dying and leaving her a widow as well as anger at some medical personnel — but this never crossed my mind, not for a second. No, anger never came into it. As it's mentioned in all the books anger in the bereaved seems to be tremendously common — Virginia Ironside's *You'll Get Over It*, in my opinion one of the best books on the subject, is subtitled *The Rage of Bereavement* — so its absence in my case might be unusual. Moreover I realise that there are some things about which it would be perfectly legitimate to be angry. That Rhona was robbed of a decade and a half, maybe two decades of life, happiness, good times, good food, beautiful places, *experience*; that she ever became ill in the first place. But there it is. Or rather, there it wasn't. Rhona's illness and death were just, as Julian Barnes puts it in *Levels of Life*, the universe doing its stuff, the universe merely doing what the universe does, which is to change its arrangement: to bring things into being and then sooner or later to destroy that arrangement. It happens to sub-atomic particles in infinitesimal slivers of a second and to galaxies over billions of years and to everything in between. Why should this species on one planet be any different?

Whatever the grievous faults of the Kübler-Ross model, and they are numerous, for me denial and depression were predominant; the other elements didn't feature. Over and above anything else, more than the denial and the depression, there was only sadness; a terrible, heart-rending, soul-tearing, wrenching sadness at my loss which has been at times almost beyond the bearing. Julian Barnes, in the book just mentioned, writes eloquently of the flat anomie that so often accompanies bereavement:

> They said the world's climate was reaching a point of no return, but it could go to that point and beyond for all it mattered to me. There is the question of anger. Some are angry with the person who has died, who has abandoned them, betrayed them by losing life. What could be more irrational than that? Few die willingly, not even most suicides. Some of the griefstruck are angry with God, but if He doesn't exist that too is irrational. Some are angry with the universe for letting

> it happen, for this being the inevitable, irreversible case. I didn't exactly feel this, but through that autumn of 2008 I read the papers and followed events on television with an overpowering indifference. 'The News' seemed just a larger, more insulting version of those busfuls of unheeding passengers, the fuel of their transport solipsism and ignorance. For some reason I cared a lot about Obama getting elected, but very little about anything else in the world. They said that the whole financial system might be about to crash and burn, but this didn't bother me. Money could not have saved her, so what good was money.

In the aftermath of Rhona's death more than one friend independently said that given the gravity of her conditions we should have had a conversation about what would happen if she was to die. The fact that we never did so — not once — is due, I am absolutely convinced and cannot be persuaded otherwise, not to any averting of the eyes from the prospect but from Rhona's rock-solid conviction that she would get better; that the valve replacement surgery would come through in time and deal with the heart failure and that she would, eventually, receive a kidney transplant. I know that some may see this as sheer denial, ridiculous pie-in-the-sky naivety; others as hopeful optimism. I deplore the glib cult of 'positive thinking' as much as the next man but I prefer to think that it was the latter; Rhona's deep love of and tenacious hold on life compelled her to see only the positives — that she had problems aplenty, certainly, but problems imply solutions and Rhona saw her problems as ones which could be and eventually would be fixed. In the last year of her life, as the aortic stenosis progressed and she fell prey to increasing fatigue and debility, having come into money after my dad's death earlier in the year I would regularly suggest buying things to make her life easier: primarily a stairlift (since getting up the stairs of our house became a particular and worsening challenge for her) and a mobility scooter. Although she had no qualms about using the latter (rented or borrowed) to get around supermarkets and town centres, for example, she steadfastly refused to countenance allowing me to buy one for her. "No", she would say politely but emphatically, again and again and again whenever the subject arose, "it'll be a waste of money, because I'm going to get better". That she *would* be better — some day; one day — became her mantra. It may have been a difficult but practical matter and perhaps those friends were right. Perhaps it's a conversation we ought to have had. The sole concession that Rhona made to what turned out to be her final illness was in acceding at the last moment to my suggestion that I make up a bed on the couch once more so that she wouldn't have to gasp and pant and haul herself up the stairs to bed, sometimes stopping half-way to sit down before regaining her breath and her strength for the last few steps. *OK. I give in!!!* she texted. This text came on the very same day that she was admitted to hospital. I didn't have time to do it; three days later I had no need to. But the fact that she caved in and agreed to it was a yielding the significance of which neither of us realised at the time. Either that, or wanted to admit.

But in the end, as I say, it wasn't a conversation we ever had. Perhaps we should have had it. Perhaps it would have made certain things just a little bit easier, just a little more straightforward when the end came. Perhaps Rhona and I should have had that talk. Perhaps she should have left behind more or less detailed instructions about what she wanted done in the event of her death. I have made detailed plans and have set certain things in place in the event of my own demise, but Rhona was not like me in that respect. Rhona loved and enjoyed life too much to want to talk about death. Rhona, unlike me, was in many ways a natural optimist. She was focused entirely and wholly and solely on life, not death. She died suddenly and *in media res*, still making plans for the future, still looking forward, still projecting herself, her life, her home into days that she would not live to see. Thanks to the inheritance I had received after my dad's death, within just weeks of Rhona's own shockingly abrupt, brutally unforeseen death we had not only drastically stepped up our dining out but had embarked on a round of alterations and improvements to our beloved nest — plush new carpets in various areas of the house; a mended kitchen roof which used to leak in heavy rain; a new shower. We were just about to start looking at wallpapers and paints for what was to be the redecorated hall, stairs and landing; we were already seeking out painters and decorators to do the job. Other necessarily short but equally luxurious breaks such as the one at Dumbleton Hall were being thought about. On the very day after she was admitted to hospital for the final time we had been due to go to the cinema to see the recently-released Queen biopic *Bohemian Rhapsody* at her instigation — a rare cinematic outing for Rhona as there were few films that she would go to the pictures to see. (I doubt that we went to the cinema much more than half a dozen times in all our years together. Once in a blue moon something piqued her interest; the previous film we had been to see had been *A Streetcat Named Bob* a couple of years previously). I had bought and reserved the tickets two days prior to her admittance to the General and she was looking forward to seeing the film, as was I. No, there was no room for thoughts of or talk about death in Rhona's future. She was going to get better.

Wasn't she?

Chapter Seventeen

Uprooted

> I have learned that if you must leave a place that you have lived in and loved and where all your yesteryears are buried deep, leave it in any way but a slow way, leave it the fastest way you can.
>
> —Beryl Markham: *West With the Night*

There is a sad coda to a sad ending of an already sad story. There is another long, complex, very difficult and painful tale altogether, but I am not minded to tell it here.

In mid-April 2019, five months after Rhona's death, I left Wareham Road and Blaby for ever, closing the door for the final time on the nest that Rhona and I had lovingly created and maintained for eighteen years, and moved back to Earl Shilton to live with an elderly aunt who was (and at time of writing still is) my last surviving relative. Unable to keep up the mortgage payments on a single meagre income (and the house being David and Leah's inheritance to boot) I bought dozens of cardboard boxes, huge rolls of bubble wrap and packed up; my hundreds, possibly thousands of books, my colossal CD collection, DVDs, kitchenware, cutlery, ornaments, sofas, TVs, the stuff of the life that Rhona and I had shared for so many years. I entertained the possibility of buying a small flat of my own but in the event the actual move was so abrupt that I had no choice but to move in, in the short term at any rate, with my aunt. Taking the two cats with me to join her there was an option; taking the dog as well was not. In floods of tears I had to let Tilly, our second Cavalier King Charles spaniel, go to another carefully vetted loving home; the second bereavement, the second crucifixion. I mowed the lawn for the final time as I had done uncountable times in the previous eighteen years, emptied the house and let Leah, as the co-executor of Rhona's will, deal with its sale. A mere five weeks after going onto the market the house in which we had lived and loved for eighteen years was sold and was taken out of my hands, out of my loving care once and for all, finally and definitively and for ever. The third crucifixion, the third bereavement in its own fashion. This was to me, on an emotional level, not like moving home (always a traumatic life event in itself on some level) but a case of squatting. Over and over and over, again and again and again, I thought: *Wo, somebody else will be living in* our *house. How can this be? How can this possibly happen?*

The home which had for eighteen years all but one day been full of voices, talk, laughter, music, light, colour, warmth, the aroma of good food became in the end a dead, empty, haunted shell. I closed the front door on it for the last time ever at 5:00pm on Friday April 12th 2019. I moved back to Earl Shilton and with the two cats moved in with my ninety year-old aunt Joan, with a bitter irony immediately next door to the house in which I had grown up which had sold just months before. Some friends — mine; Rhona's; shared friends — helpfully and hopefully saw this as the opportunity to start a new chapter in my life. I appreciated the sentiment behind it but couldn't and still can't share it; but as far as I'm concerned really there is no new chapter for the bereft and the grieving, only changes of circumstance whether consciously chosen or (as in this case) enforced. Many of the bereavement books I read and many bereavement counsellors opine that after a devastating loss such as a bereavement no serious, life-changing decisions (new relationship; new home, possibly in an altogether different area; new job and so on) should be made for a year at the very least and perhaps longer — some say two years. But in my case I had no choice in the matter. I didn't want or choose to leave; I had to. I always knew that it would have to come at some point but the final departure came suddenly with little to no chance to absorb the fact of the uprooting from the home, from the neighbourhood, from the village, from the *life* that Rhona and I had created together and all the things with which we had filled our days.

Inevitably, given my precipitate departure, I took as much of the stuff of our life together as I was able to take with me. Most of it went into (and at time of writing remains in) long-term storage but I took with me to Earl Shilton as much of the everyday items of our life as I could manage. Rhona's favourite white bullet mug, our best knives and other well-used and even loved kitchen utensils, baking trays, cutlery, bedding, cushions, our rickety but familiar sewing box, innumerable other things I won't list. I saved much of the clothing that Rhona had worn in the closing months of her life and which features in so many photographs. At time of this writing, not quite ten months after her death, the collar of her beloved black and hot pink Simply Be anorak, seen in so many of the aforementioned photos and now kept in darkness in the loft, still smelt — still *smells*; I am writing very much in the present tense here — of shampoo and of Estée Lauder's Beautiful (her favourite perfume, launched in 1985 and still one of the company's biggest sellers). Still smelt — still *smells* —, in short, of Rhona. Other items of Rhona's clothing that I kept, ones which she wore regularly in the last months, weeks, days of her life, still bear that scent. Doubtless given enough time, perhaps by the time this account sees the light of day it will slowly fade away and finally disappear; this is inevitable and inevitably excruciating. In his novel *A Prayer for Owen Meany* John Irving wrote:

> When someone you love dies, and you're not expecting it, you don't lose her all at once; you lose her in pieces over a long time—the way the mail stops coming, and her scent fades from the pillows and even from the clothes in her closet and drawers. Gradually, you accumulate the parts of her that are gone. Just when the day comes—when there's a particular missing

> part that overwhelms you with the feeling that she's gone, forever—there comes another day, and another specifically missing part.

That may be to come; but for now it is still there. Everybody knows how powerfully and even painfully evocative scents can be: more than three quarters of a year after her passing the coat and the other clothing still carries Rhona's smell. I bought a bottle of her perfume to carry around with me in my coat pocket, not to wear but to sniff from time to time to remind myself of what had always been the scent of a very particular and specific woman. I did the same with Badedas shower gel, another of Rhona's aromas — day to day she was a shower person but every so often she would opt for a brutally hot bath, which she would ask me to run, into which I would add a generous dose of her favourite Badedas bath gelee. It was vital for me to do these things because, although at the time I'd said nothing and had kept my thoughts very much to myself, I'd been grievously dismayed and upset by what I felt was the unseemly haste with which my dad — an unsentimental man, entirely unlike me — had got rid of my mum's clothes and other belongings after her death in August 2001. Doubtless it was his practical and hands-on way of managing his own grief but it seemed to me to be unfeeling, cold, even on the callous side, as though the stuff of my mum's life could be quickly dispensed with, exactly as I would later feel about the clearance of our home in Wareham Road. I was not going to follow suit.

Perhaps some would see this as unhealthy — a trying to cling onto or even to recreate something of life in Blaby — but people handle their grief (if they handle it at all) in different ways and this was my way of, yes, hanging onto life with Rhona in some fashion. Healthy or unhealthy, be that as it may, it's what I did. The Buddhists tell us in the second of what's known as the Four Noble Truths that fundamentally the root of all suffering is attachment. Well, I've had a deep and serious interest in Buddhism for many years and, like Judaism, have amassed a fair library of books on the subject. But even though there is much to admire and respect in Buddhism (I've pursued basically Buddhist meditation for years, for example) I'm not a Buddhist and don't agree with, don't even *like*, large swathes of its philosophy. A life lived without attachment doesn't sound like any kind of life that I'm interested in living. If the Buddhists are right and it's the case that the basis of suffering is attachment, on balance I think I'd sooner take the attachment and bear the consequences of the suffering that goes with it. I'll take the attachment and the suffering in spite of knowing the pain that it will bring because that pain is the price we must pay when we lose those people in life that we love the most, and we love them the most because they *matter*. Good luck with Buddhism if that's what roasts your potatoes and it may be that I fundamentally misunderstand the concept of non-attachment, but non-attachment, especially to beloved people that we know we can always lose at potentially any time, doesn't sound to me like any goal that I want to pursue.

Within a few weeks of moving back to Earl Shilton I too suffered a fairly steep decline in my health, including prostate and urinary problems, frighteningly swollen feet and ankles that took me to Leicester Royal Infirmary at midnight and even a disturbed cardiac rhythm traced to a silent heart attack which I'd had at some unknown, unspecified point in the past, picked up by an ECG during a comprehensive medical assessment. I'd had no idea that there was such a thing as a SMI — a silent myocardial infarction — but the doctor with whom I discussed my test results explained they're much more common than generally believed and can sometimes be every bit as dangerous as the more obvious heart attack; the 'silent' part comes from the fact that it disguises itself as anything that makes you feel ill but not obviously experiencing cardiac problems. It can hide as a panic attack. It can hide as what feels like an incipient bout of flu. In women especially, I was told, it can be camouflaged as what's taken to be a bad case of indigestion. This may have been coincidental and may have happened anyway — I'm the 'right' sex and more or less in the 'right' age group; scare quotes entirely deliberate — or it may have been the essentially self-inflicted outcome of too much grief, too little food, too much stress, too little self-care, too much booze, too little sleep. I have no idea. In any case this is a part of the tale I won't go into, certainly not because I have some sort of personal objection to doing so but because it can't be of any interest to anyone else and is becoming, I increasingly think, of dwindling interest even to myself.

In May 2019 I marked — I won't say celebrated — my forty-seventh birthday, the first birthday in twenty-one years without Rhona. And then, almost eight months after her death — Thursday July 4th 2019; a very warm, dry, balmy and sunny summer's day — Joan and I made the long, hot, arduous journey by train from Leicester to Stevenage via Peterborough which as a young man I had done so many times two decades earlier and to Weston Road cemetery to visit all too briefly the grave on what would have been, could have been, *should* have been Rhona's sixty-eighth birthday, placing a bouquet of yellow roses on the spot in which she rests. The plot, last seen by me on the bleakest, grimmest, greyest of wet, tempestuous winter days, was now lightly covered in sparse young grass and bathed in warm summer sunshine.

Two days before leaving Wareham Road, before leaving Blaby, I visited — presumably for the last time ever — the steakhouse not far away which had become Rhona's favourite place to eat in the final year of her life and which gave her so much delight, as attested to by so many lovely photographs showing a beaming, beautiful woman enjoying her food, some of the best photographs of her ever taken. I went alone for lunch (though as a life-long vegetarian and aspiring vegan not for a steak, obviously) and sat in a booth where we had sat many a time in the past; going there, where we had been so many times in those final months, with someone, anyone else was unthinkable. As I prepared to leave I told myself that I was leaving Blaby for the last time ever; that I would not be able to cope emotionally with revisiting the village/town which had been our home for so many years. I don't know if that will remain the case for ever — it may; it may not. I don't know. I have a terrible longing to return; I miss Blaby generally and our house in Wareham Road dreadfully but am not — yet — emotionally prepared to revisit. Again, that may change in the future, but for now it would be too raw, too painful an experience to go back to the place where Rhona and I shared our life for nearly twenty years. I've been abroad only once and have no desire anymore to repeat the experience; once I'd hoped to see Israel as Rhona did shortly before she became ill, but the fact is that my travelling days are over. Still: on a more local level one day, if and when I don't feel as though I have been flayed alive, I hope to take a sentimental journey back to as many of the places that Rhona and I visited as I possibly can, one by one. I have friends and family that I love dearly but this is something that I will have to do without them. No offence, but no one else is invited; this one is just for me and Rhona.

Chapter Eighteen

Kaddish

> I hope when I die I shan't leave such cruel gaps in other people's lives.
>
> —Ralph Partridge to Frances Partridge, February 15th 1932

At the beginning of his memoir *Speak, Memory* Vladimir Nabokov mentions a young man of his acquaintance who suffered from chronophobia, the morbid fear of the passage of time, an unusual, uncommon but by no means unknown condition. According to Nabokov this young man was brought to a state of something akin to panic when viewing home movies made a few weeks before his birth. "He saw a world that was practically unchanged — the same house, the same people — and then realized that he did not exist there at all and that nobody mourned his absence."

I understand this only too well. I have more than a mild case of chronophobia myself and to me one of the more distressing aspects of grief is the knowledge that each passing day takes me further away from the reality of the living, breathing, laughing, eBaying, TV-watching, radio-listening, steak-loving, salad-eating, coffee-drinking human being that Rhona once was who now exists only in photographs and in videos (not nearly enough of either, though in the case of photographs they must run into the hundreds. Still not enough) and in memory. All chronophobics are by definition obsessively consumed by the passage of time and what time consumes (*tempus edax rerum* as Ovid put it; time devours everything). If, as some have opined, all fears stem *au fond* from the fear of death and the nothingness (if it is) into which not only we ourselves but everything familiar to us must sooner or later fall, chronophobia would seem to be an example of this fear in its rawest form. I would like to be able to say what is doubtless considered to be the emotionally healthy thing, that I see each new day as a fresh start and another opportunity for good things in life, but as a naturally melancholic character with a view of life which can be described as downbeat at best and at worst frankly bleak I see only one day further away from a living Rhona … though there may be a counter-argument to that, which I shall mention at the end of this chapter.

To be bereaved is to be robbed. Quite literally: etymologically, the word, which first came into everyday usage in the eighteenth century, is based on *reave* which ultimately comes from the Old English *rēafian*, meaning to rob, to plunder, to steal. To be bereaved is to have something — some*one* — stolen from you, taken by force. Anything taken from us against our will — a car; a wallet; a treasured possession — brings about a form of grief, and when the thing that is stolen from us is the person dearer to us and loved by us more than any other then the grief is correspondingly worse. To have our home burgled, to have a car nicked, to be pickpocketed, is to have our innate human belief in some ultimate, cosmic form of fairness and justice — what's known in psychology as the just world hypothesis — violated. This is not right; this is breaking the rules; this is unfair, we feel, and we are naturally outraged. How great the outrage and sense of injustice, then, when the person we love most in the world is taken from us, especially prematurely or in a sudden manner.

The blunter and more brutal — because more realistic and honest — books on bereavement, grief and mourning say that in some catastrophic ways for some people and in certain ways for everyone grief is never over. Acceptance — whatever that may look like; if it comes at all in some form since for some it never does so — can only ever be partial. The story of devastating loss is never quite done until we as individuals are also done with. And one day we *will* be done with, every one of us. Some of the aforementioned books also relate the bleak truth that for at least some of the bereaved there isn't a gradual lessening of grief and that the second year after a devastating loss can be if anything even harder than the first. Julian Barnes, in his short and beautiful hybrid work *Levels of Life*, writes (of the death of his wife Pat):

> You think that Year Two can't be worse than Year One, and imagine yourself prepared for it. You think you have met all the different sorts of pain you will be asked to bear, and that after this there will only be repetition. But why should repetition mean less pain?

If there can be accumulation of love over the years, he continues, *then why not of grief?* A minority (albeit a relatively substantial minority; somewhere between 10 and 20% according to some studies) of the bereaved find themselves experiencing the horrors of what is known as complicated grief, more technically and clinically known in the literature as persistent complex bereavement disorder (PCBD). This is where the symptoms of grief do not gradually lessen and soften somewhat with the passage of time (as most people find eventually, even though the pain of loss remains) but remain as fresh and as horrifically raw as in the immediate aftermath of loss or even, in the very worst of cases, get worse. While every experience of grief is of course unique to the individual, much research indicates that complicated grief can start to be identified about six months after a bereavement; people suffering from complicated grief or PCBD remain obsessively, relentlessly preoccupied with memories of the one who has been lost to an unusually intense degree not associated with 'simple' grief; they have either an extreme concentration upon things associated with them or, alternatively, an almost phobic aversion to anything associated with them. They may find it impossible to accept that the death has truly, actually happened; they may feel numb, bitter or angry; utterly bleak despair and hopelessness about the future can lead to thoughts of — or even attempts at — suicide; above all else the grief is and remains so intense and unbearable that a return to normal life becomes impossible. In short, complicated grievers become 'stuck' in a grief which doesn't ease as the weeks turn into months and then years. While everybody acknowledges that a great deal more research is needed to try to understand why some people suffer complicated as opposed to 'simple' grief (as though there could ever be anything simple about it) it's known that several factors make its development more likely — pre-existing mental health conditions such as depression and anxiety (check); misuse of alcohol and other drugs (check); an exceptionally close and dependent relationship with the one who has died (check); a sudden, traumatic or premature death (such as by murder, suicide or sudden illness for instance; check) amongst them; alternatively a difficult, troubled or fraught relationship or one which ended abruptly with many loose ends left untied. In actual fact the brains of those suffering from complicated grief literally operate in a different manner to those with 'simple' grief in a surprising way; as hard as it may be to believe, neurological research has demonstrated that complicated grief brings its sufferers as much pleasure as it does agony by operating on the brain centres — specifically the limbic system and the nucleus accumbens, if we're being precise — responsible for pleasure, reward and addiction. Counter-intuitive as it may be but complicated grievers are addicted to their grief as much as alcoholics are to vodka and gamblers to fruit machines and betting shops, which is why it is so difficult to treat.

Although not due to a literal death, after being jilted on her wedding day Miss Havisham in Dickens's *Great Expectations* can be thought of as a fictional example of complicated grief, stalled for ever in her loss, her wedding dress falling to rags on her body, the wedding cake being eaten by mice on the table and all the clocks in Satis House stopped at exactly the moment when she first heard that she had been spurned. Arguably Queen Victoria, who wore black to the end of her days and had Prince Albert's clothes laid out on the bed each morning, was a real-life example of the same phenomenon. The DSM-5 — the fifth edition of the *Diagnostic and Statistical Manual of Mental Disorders*, the 'bible' of the American Psychiatric Association — does not yet recognise PCBD as a psychological disorder in its own right but has placed it in its 'Conditions for Further Study' section. This is controversial; many experts in the field resist what they see as medicalising a normal and natural reaction to terrible loss — almost any and every facet of human experience seems to have the word 'disorder' tacked onto it these days. Even so, there's little doubt that complicated grief, akin in some respects to a form of post-traumatic stress, is a profoundly debilitating condition which devastates or even destroys lives, causes unimaginable suffering and is notoriously difficult to treat. It responds poorly to antidepressants, although some progress may be made with psychotherapy specifically targeted at PCBD.

These are hard, harsh, ugly, unpalatable truths for some, things that nobody wants to hear. But books, like lives, must have an end; and I now have to find, somehow, some sort of conclusion to a story which I still write and will continue to write, both literally and figuratively, every day of the existence that remains to me.

It goes without saying that Rhona should never have become ill and should still be here today, living and loving her life as she did. Platitude it may be but sixty-seven is no age; trying to extract something at least slightly positive from it all it could be said that dying at the age at which she did Rhona was spared the indignities and infirmities of old age, though I would have cared for her through all these as well, being so many years — two decades — younger than she was. She could have depended on that. I hoped for it. Rhona was almost twenty-one years my senior so, barring accident or illness, I suppose I should have always expected that she would go first. Oddly, though, for some reason as I've previously said, I always felt that I would be the one to go first, hence the fact that on the very day that she was admitted to hospital I was about to visit my solicitor to make my will in Rhona's favour; and in any case Rhona would have inherited longevity genes from her parents. Her much-loved father Leslie died suddenly but peacefully in 2010 aged eighty; at time of writing her mother lives on still, close to ninety. Death, perhaps especially sudden death, is such a savage and brutal irruption into everyday life for a multitude of reasons but one of those reasons — one of the major reasons — is that it puts a final and definitive closure to any hopes for the future, a decisive terminus for any plans, a door slammed shut on *what we're going to do next*; all the things never to be done, all the places never to be seen, all the words that now can never be said. Rhona, unlike me, was a basically optimistic, upbeat and positive person who looked to the future. She expected to have and to see one; despite the seriousness of her conditions we both thought that she would live to see the seventies and eighties which should have been hers by right. In *Love, Interrupted* Simon Thomas points out that in the UK (at the time of the deaths of his wife and of Rhona, just a year apart) the average life expectancy for a woman is 82.9 years. Thomas's wife Gemma died in November 2017 at the age of only forty, less than half of the average; clearly Rhona was much nearer to it and yet, since statistically women live longer than men, in the normal course of events a healthy Rhona could have expected to have looked forward to a decade and a half of further life or even, had she taken after her mum, very considerably more.

Because we had such a disparity in age we were never, like equally-aged couples, going to expect to grow into extreme old age together; in the months after Rhona's death the sight of elderly couples — elderly couples especially; elderly couples in particular —, some of them holding hands as they ambled along, filled me with a cold, wretched despair; certainly not anger, not quite even envy *per se*, but an overwhelming sorrow. That was us once — that was us recently — and should have been us in the future, age gap or no. Rhona at eighty would have found me at sixty, as unimaginable an age to me now as forty-seven surely was at twenty. But we did hope and expect to grow old*er* together in spite of my inexplicable feeling that it would be me who departed first. In the event sickness overtook her, which as I say should never have occurred.

The uncomfortable counterpart to that however is that if she *hadn't* got ill I would possibly never have returned to Blaby, would never have resumed our relationship and would never have had the honour and the privilege — the greatest I'll ever know, that's for sure — of being able to care for her in what turned out to be the final three and a half years of her life. Granted, it may have happened anyway, but of that I can never be certain. In my unfortunate affair of 2011 I betrayed the love and trust Rhona had invested in me for the previous thirteen years and caused her tremendous hurt and I shall regret this bitterly to my last breath. The guilt and shame of that will never leave me, which may not be healthy from an emotional, psychological point of view but is a fact all the same. Couples who are together for a long time can, almost inevitably, get to a point where they take each other, the sheer daily presence of the other, for granted. It's unfortunate but, as I say, perhaps almost inescapable. That said, it's my belief that even after my betrayal, the reason that Rhona and I came back together and remained together and put so much effort into our relationship is that we had both grown up as the children of very long, loving, happy and successful marriages. Commitment — serious, genuine, lasting commitment — came naturally to us; we had had the template for it instilled in us by our respective sets of parents. Hers were married for slightly less than fifty years; mine for almost forty. We both knew exactly what a long-lasting marriage looked like and what it entailed. We were primed for it; we knew better than to casually throw away something so rich, something so wonderful, something so enduring. The opportunity to care for Rhona in her last few years, all the tending to her needs — the washing, the dressing, the undressing, the feeding, the accompaniment to so many, many hospital appointments, the pushing her around in a wheelchair and maybe especially the opportunity to lay my own life on the line for her not once but twice in attempting to donate a kidney — perhaps went some way to repairing some of the damage I had so selfishly, so thoughtlessly inflicted on what was our *de facto* if not *de jure* marriage. How far this repair went is not for me to judge. I am in no position to say; Rhona didn't vocalise it explicitly. Then again perhaps she did … in her final birthday card to me ("When it comes to being special," reads the message on the front and inside, "You're the specialist!") in May 2018 she wrote in her instantly recognisable looping handwriting that I was her "specialist [*sic*] bestest [*sic*] friend and partner, carer and companion, from an ever grateful, not-very-able, faithful but demanding Rhona XXXX." Rhona had not always been noted for her diligence in remembering to send greetings cards (a few Christmases and birthdays passed without one from her to me — I didn't mind; it was just Rhona being Rhona) so this last one was and is and will ever remain exceptionally special. There will never be another birthday card or any other kind of card from Rhona but I consider that that message will do nicely in standing in for all the other birthdays I may have, however many of them there may be left to me.

Although frequently frightening, sometimes desperately sad and more often than not challenging to say the least of it, the years of Rhona's illness — I should say illnesses — also had so many, many moments of deep tenderness, amazing beauty, unconditional love and sheer, incredible magic that, weighed in the balance, I would not have missed them for anything in the world. Metal and glass are annealed by fire; relationships, if they are not ultimately destroyed by it, are tested by adversity. It may be financial or familial adversity but there is no test of a relationship so testing as a health crisis that comes out of a clear blue sky; the lump discovered where there shouldn't be a lump, the cough that just won't go away, blood where there shouldn't be blood. Those times lifted our relationship onto an altogether different plane, one of a greater love on my part and a greater intimacy for both of us than I think we had ever previously known. Rhona was in her own way a heroine, far and away not merely the best but also the bravest person I have ever known. There is a common saying online: 'Not all heroes wear capes'. Certainly the medical staff I met in these three and a half final years qualify as heroes in my mind (although I've known some medical practitioners to bridle at the term, preferring to be acknowledged as professionals doing a demanding job in difficult circumstances) but it applies to Rhona too. I can say for a certain fact that faced with what was landed on her plate there is no way in the world that I would ever demonstrate such quiet, stoical, uncomplaining courage. I was and am so proud of her; for her grit, her tough-mindedness, her sheer bloody-minded fortitude, her utter lack of self-pity, the balls she demonstrated (what Americans such as Mark Twain more politely call *sand*) in having things done to her — some highly disagreeable, some scary and some downright painful things — that I, craven coward that I am about all things medical, would never in a million years have had done to me; the dignity, even nobility with which she dealt with her illnesses; her humour in some dark and extremely trying days; her ability still to enjoy small but infinitely precious things and to extract joy from her days as her life force slowly waned.

I just wish that these experiences, these qualities, had come about for other reasons. Of course.

So much of life is ruled by randomness, and most people are afraid of randomness since randomness equals an absence of the (as far as I'm concerned, mostly illusory) control we think we have over most of our lives. Scientifically we know this to be true in the quantum world; it's also true in the human world. The sheer unlikeliness of our life together still boggles my mind. I might never have bought a computer and introduced myself to the internet. Even if I had, I might never have met Caron and Nigel Eagling. Even if I had, they might never have introduced me to Rhona. Even if they had, Rhona might never have suggested that she and I meet up. Even if we had, we might never have had anything more than a single night of passion. Even if we had, I might never have gone down to Stevenage and in effect made it my home overnight. All these things happened and so many, many, many more; but they need not have happened. It could all have been so very, very different for the both of us. At any and every point the universe could have taken us in different, random directions altogether, splitting and bifurcating and ramifying into alternate histories, other timelines in the way that proponents of the many-worlds interpretation of quantum mechanics believe it does; but somehow it threw Rhona and me together and the rest as they say is history — her story; my story; our story; *this* story. Although it never bothered me in the slightest (I only ever felt immense gratitude at my good fortune) I was always perfectly well aware that Rhona and I were an amazingly unusual pairing — difference in background; the age gap of course — and from time to time Rhona would marvel at the inherent unlikeliness, the sheer implausibility of our ever having even met at all let alone become a couple for what would eventually be over two decades. "Do you think the universe fights for souls to be together?" pondered the poet Emery Allen. "Some things are too strange and strong to be coincidences." The sheer improbability of our meeting and the implausibility of our story still baffles me; some people search all their lives and either never find or lose what I fell into by utterly random accident.

Well, perhaps.

Always considered a confirmed bachelor — he had long derided the institution of marriage (which he called "the end of hope") and held disobliging views about women in general — the great American journalist H. L. Mencken surprised many by marrying the author and academic Sara Haardt in 1930 after a seven-year courtship. To the astonishment of many (most of all, one suspects, to Mencken himself) it was a devoted love-match but one which was to be cut cruelly short due to Sara's death from meningitis — a complication of long-standing tuberculosis — in May 1935 aged just thirty-seven. On the fifth anniversary of her death Mencken wrote in his diary what I think of as some of the most beautiful prose about a happy marriage that I know, every bit of which is applicable to the relationship, marriage in all but the legal sense, that Rhona and I had for more than four times as long:

> Sara is dead five years today—a longer time than the time of our marriage, which lasted but four years and nine months. It is amazing what a deep mark she left upon my life—and yet, after all, it is not amazing at all, for a happy marriage throws out numerous and powerful tentacles. They may loosen with years and habit, but when a marriage ends at the height of its success they endure. It is a literal fact that I still think of Sara every day of my life, and almost every hour of the day. Whenever I see anything that she would have liked I find myself saying that I'll buy it and take it to her, and I am always thinking of things to tell her [...] I can recall no single moment during our years together when I ever had the slightest doubt of our marriage, or wished it had never been. I believe that she was equally content. We had our troubles, especially her illnesses, but they never set up any difference between us: they always drew us closer and closer together [...]

> Marriage is largely talk, and I still recall clearly the long palavers we used to have [...] We had plenty to talk of. I talked out my projects with her, and she talked out hers with me. I don't think we ever bored each other. I know that, for my part, the last days of that gabbling were as stimulating as the first [...] I have never known a more rational woman, nor another half so charming [...] Thinking of her, I can well understand the great human yearning for immortality, but I do not believe in it, and neither did she [...] I'll have her in mind until thought and memory adjourn, but that is all. Whether or not it is better so I do not know, but there is the fact as I see it. We were happy together, but all beautiful things must end.

Mencken was shattered by Sara's death and in many respects, cliché or not, never fully recovered from it. In 1950 one of the greatest masters of the American language suffered a catastrophic stroke and for the last six years of his life he was unable to read, unable to write and had great difficulty in speaking. His last few years were spent listening to music, until his own life came to a close.

Also cliché or not, Rhona was, is and ever will be the love of my lifetime. Many of the bereavement memoirs that I worked my way through in the wake of Rhona's death end with the writer embarking eventually upon a new relationship; some brief, some enduring, sometimes even a new marriage. I'm always happy that people find happiness anew; but that happiness is at something of a remove and, I have to say, is in my case somewhat qualified. It's not for me. I am wary of going into this too deeply and am choosing my words very carefully indeed because if handled badly it will make me look purse-lipped, censorious and disapproving, Mrs Grundy-ish, and I don't believe for one moment that I am. I begrudge no one happiness in seeking and finding love again after shattering loss, but for me personally, and bearing in mind the old adage that it's never wise to say never, I couldn't, can't countenance the thought of a new relationship. No ... no ... no, not after what Rhona and I had for so many years. In the Egyptian tradition with which she became so familiar — as in many traditional cultures — widows are expected to remain widows for the rest of their days (widowers not so much, unsurprisingly) and on the whole that's a tradition that I understand. Clearly I'm glad (such a limp, feeble word in the circumstances …) that Rhona didn't take the same attitude or we would never have met, but we had different views on lots of things, though the same views on much more. Apparently research has shown that widowers remarry much more often — as much as ten times more often — and faster than do widows; studies have revealed that the average time between the death of a wife and remarriage is two and a half years, and the younger the widower and the happier he was married the sooner he is likely to start dating and to remarry. Men, it would seem, find it much harder to live without a wife than the opposite case. I'm mildly, slightly, vicariously glad for those who feel able to do it; there's grief and sorrow and misery and loneliness enough in this world and happiness has to be grabbed with both hands wherever it can be found. But again, it's not for me. Perhaps I have rigid or old-fashioned views in this area — I probably do — but a new relationship would seem, firstly, like an attempt at replacing the utterly irreplaceable and secondly like an emotional betrayal. I have been too badly burnt by the shame, guilt and remorse of infidelity to risk that a second time; but more importantly, very close to twenty-one of the best years of my life were shared with Rhona. The vacancy is closed and nobody else need apply. Rhona was the love of my life, my first and only serious long-term relationship — marriage in all but the legal sense — and I intend to keep it that way. I've no doubt that these days the Queen Victoria approach (life-long mourning and permanent widow's weeds, so beautifully captured in Helen Rappaport's *Magnificent Obsession*, an enthralling study in what was clearly a case of complicated grief) is viewed as deeply unhealthy, damaging and maladaptive, but in all honesty it's something that I fully understand, respect and even — I will go ahead and say it; sue me — admire. In hanging on to so many of the artefacts of our life together (some of Rhona's clothing; ornaments; even kitchen utensils) I've wondered if I have ever been, was, *am* in danger of falling into complicated grief. (Meghan O'Rourke: "Holding on indefinitely to the possessions of the dead, or keeping rooms just as the dead left them, are symptoms of complicated or pathological grief, I'd learned"). I'm not a specialist in the area and not in a position to say. I don't especially care; for all that I'm reasonably knowledgeable on the subject and sufficiently self-aware to know that I tick some of the boxes, I'm not big on the sometimes self-serving, sometimes self-aggrandising and always self-interested business of self-diagnosis. 'Simple' grief', 'complicated' grief … who cares, really? Grief is grief is grief. It's all grief to me.

For years I have been haunted — obsessed would hardly be too strong a word — by the ancient Greek myth of Orpheus, the preternaturally-gifted musician who descended to the underworld to bring back his beloved wife Eurydice. It exists in various subtly different versions, although arguably the ur-version is found in Ovid's *Metamorphoses*. The story has similarly obsessed Western artists ever since, spawning countless works of art of every type: poetry (Rilke's *Sonnets to Orpheus* being perhaps the most celebrated example), music (Gluck's *Orfeo ed Euridice* likewise), painting, sculpture, film, even video games and comics. The basic version of the tale is that Orpheus, son of Apollo and the muse Calliope, meets, falls in love with and marries the beautiful Eurydice. On their wedding day Orpheus played joyful music on his lyre while Eurydice danced. In Virgil's version Eurydice was lusted after by the shepherd Aristaeus who made advances to her; fleeing in alarm Eurydice trod on a snake, was bitten and died. A devastated Orpheus took up his lyre and sang songs of such tragic, wrenching beauty that all humans and even the gods were deeply moved. Orpheus decided to descend to the shadowy underworld of ancient Greek belief to plead with Hades and Persephone, rulers of the lower realms, to allow him to bring Eurydice back to the land of the living. Orpheus made his case so affectingly that Hades agreed but on one condition; Orpheus must walk in front of Eurydice and must on no account turn around to look at her until both were safely back in the upper world or Eurydice would return to the underworld and be lost for ever. Orpheus began to lead Eurydice back to life, but in a moment of doubt he turned around to see if his wife was still following and, exactly as ordained by Hades, she faded back into the underworld. No mortal can enter Hades twice while he lives, and a despairing Orpheus was torn apart by frenzied Maenads (literally 'the raving ones'), his severed head kept by the Muses still singing laments of unspeakable beauty. As noted, the story has been a potent source of inspiration for innumerable artists for two thousand years; the tragic tale of a man so in love with his wife that he will dare the infernal realms — death itself — to win her back continues to inspire. Its appeal to any widower with more than a passing interest in Greek mythology is too obvious to labour the point.

Thomas Mann once defined a writer as someone for whom writing is more difficult than it is for other people, a dismal but accurate definition I have too often ruefully pondered. Concluding this account I realise more than ever before how poor are words to convey the life of two people together for so long and a love of the kind that we had; a love of that intensity; that length and breadth and height and depth. Of making many books there is no end, it says in one book; but no book can hope to completely and accurately convey the reality of two people living and loving together for a very long time. After tens of thousands of words I realise dismally that I'm not a good enough writer to be able to convey to the reader the specifics and particularities of a specific and particular person, the myriad things that make someone who and what they are and not someone else — how Rhona liked her coffee (strong; one spoon of Coffeemate Light as well as milk; two sugars); the love of rare steaks; how she smelt of shampoo and of her favourite perfume (Estée Lauder's Beautiful) and loved almost scaldingly hot baths, run by me, with Badedas bubble bath, the scent of both of these things instantly evoking Rhona; how she loved preparing and eating a huge plate of salad; her addiction to tomatoes, butter ("Do you want some bread to go with that butter?" was a familiar if unoriginal refrain in our house), Wotsits and Huthwaite's Edwardian mints; the passion for listening to LBC (the voices of Nick Ferrari, James O'Brien and Shelagh Fogarty will stay with me to the day I die); the time and care she lavished on doing and redoing her nails; how she made cheese on toast — her fast go-to breakfast — with lots of chopped red onion and a generous dousing of Lea and Perrins Worcestershire sauce; her love of the kitschy camp of the Eurovision Song Contest (every year we would have a sheet of paper and a pen each, marking every song and comparing scores at the end); how she meticulously peeled off the skins of potatoes and tomatoes (to me the best bit) before eating the flesh; the love of shopping; the many television programmes she relished (I still can't bring myself to watch *Bargain Hunt* and *Gogglebox*; the memories are too painful); her huge collection of home design magazines; her squeamish horror of fictitious screen violence but fascination with true crime, both in print and on television; her habit of unconsciously twizzling her already curly hair into Topsy-knots while watching television … what I mean here is the sheer *Rhona*-ness of one particular person out of seven billion with whom I had the unbelievable fortune and privilege of sharing almost a third of her life. I could, if I chose, multiply specific examples almost endlessly. An item-by-item of everything about my and Rhona's life together — a list of memories — would make the *Encyclopaedia Britannica* look like a note for the milkman by comparison; but for one thing they would be meaningless and more than likely tedious to anyone but myself (it matters hugely to me that Rhona loved a prawn korma and *Strictly Come Dancing* but what does it signify to anyone else?) and for another, I know that all attempts to convey this essence of Rhona-ness to those who never had the inexpressibly good fortune to have met her are doomed to failure.

To say that I learnt or discovered nothing from the experience of losing Rhona would be inaccurate. Unfortunately many of these discoveries are things that nobody — nobody — should ever have to uncover. That there is a depth of suffering, pain, sorrow, sadness and loneliness incomprehensible until and unless one experiences it directly; that great grief is the price to be paid for great love; that loss and the pain that accompanies it are inevitable in life unless one dies early; the mystery of time; the persistence and pain of memory; that life is utterly uncontrollable and unpredictable and so very, very precarious that the very best and the very worst of things happen randomly in the blink of an eye. It may be that in this life nothing comes free and that everything ultimately has to be bought and paid for; that the misery and agony of these days, weeks and months is the price I now have to pay for our many years of happiness. You cannot, as far as I'm concerned, 'make friends' with grief in the way that I've seen some self-help authors recommend that their readers try to 'make friends' with depression or anxiety or whatever. And nor should you. There's nothing friendly about grief. It's nobody's friend. The exact opposite, in fact. It's a foul, hideous, horrible, ghastly thing. The very best you can hope for, in my opinion, is some sort of coolly distant but manageable working relationship on a daily basis.

Even in a post-Christian world so many of us still seem to be prey to the notion, old but still lingering about the collective consciousness, that suffering is somehow redemptive; that to suffer is to go through a process at the end of which one emerges purified — more patient, more noble, more stoical, more understanding, simply *better.* This seems to me to be a flagrant delusion; while this may very well be true in some cases I can't see any reason why suffering isn't equally likely to make someone crabbed, cramped, narrow, angry, embittered and despairing. In *The Widower's Notebook* Jonathan Santlofer, as ever, nails it:

> Something I am loath to admit: that the loss of my wife did not make me a stronger, better, or more enlightened person. [...] loss remains a part of you, a hole or a void that you will carry forever, no matter how you try to fill it [...]
>
> Do we overcome grief?
>
> The answer, for me, is not really. Grief is a permanent scar, part of who I am now and who I always will be. There are certain things we are not meant to get over and the loss of our nearest and dearest is, I believe, in that category. But it does not have to kill us (at least not yet).

In their anthology *The Book of Love and Loss: Poems for Today* the editors R. V. Bailey and June Hall write:

> Love and loss must surely be the most significant experiences in most people's lives. Neither can be predicted, and neither, perhaps, avoided. The first is altogether life-enhancing; to be able to love someone, and to be loved by that someone — these things set the world on fire. You are blessed beyond words. Simply because you are human, you may know love [...] But once you know love, you are doomed. For you are a hostage to fortune: the greater the love, the greater the grief of loss, and just as suddenly, the world can change again. To lose that pearl of great price, having once so miraculously found it, is a mortal blow [...] happiness, as you knew it — have known it, perhaps, for a lifetime — has gone for ever.

Some traditional societies and cultures around the world (where, for example, arranged marriage might be practiced) have on occasion charged we in the West with making too much of romantic love, saying that personal attraction, subject as it is to fading over time, disappearing outright or being transferred to another person, is too fickle, too precarious, too arbitrary a basis for a secure and enduring relationship. A cursory glance at the latest divorce statistics may lead you to think that they might have a point. Yet Bailey and Hall are to my mind perfectly correct: most people in most places most of the time find romantic relationships — a loving and intimate union with one other person, a true meeting of hearts and minds — to be the richest, most rewarding and fulfilling experiences of their entire lives beside which the daily round of getting and spending, the achievements of career, fame and fortune, are as nothing. There is nothing admirable in being an unloved, loveless and lonely billionaire and, twee and clichéd as a cheap greeting card as it may unavoidably sound, the person who has found true, lasting love of the deepest kind — some never do — has won first prize in the lottery of life. However many divorces there may be, most human beings continue to chase after their ideal of the perfect relationship which, though it may be a fantasy, is pursued for a reason; namely that most people recognise that intimate relationships, however often they go wrong and cause emotional carnage, when they go right provide the greatest happiness and satisfaction we ever know in this world. There is even a medical aspect to this; it's been known for decades that happily partnered people statistically suffer fewer mental and physical illnesses and even that married men live longer than those who are not. (Though this effect isn't replicated in married women for unknown reasons, and in any case statistically women live longer than men anyway. Old gag: why do husbands die earlier than their wives? Because they want to. I don't find this quite as funny as I used to, somehow).

In the Jewish tradition there is a phrase commonly heard when speaking about a deceased female which by sheer happy coincidence contains Rhona's name and which I have used as one of the epigraphs to this book: *zikhronah livrakhah* — may her memory be a blessing. Rhona's presence was the greatest blessing of my life and her memory will be the greatest blessing of my remaining days, however many they may be.

The Talmud — that vast compendious repository of Jewish lore, commentary, counter-commentary, argument, counter-argument, counter-counter-argument and counter-counter-counter-argument — famously says that whoever kills a person kills an entire world, the corollary to which is that an entire life is an entire world. Whenever someone dies a world dies with them; a world — their world — of thought and feeling, of memory and experience which, no matter the diaries, the letters, the photograph albums, the video footage, the emails, the text messages, is impossible to retrieve or replicate fully. Since Rhona's death I have dwelt upon that long and hard and I fear often very bitterly. For twenty-one years Rhona's world and mine were not so much intertwined as the same thing; faithfully recorded as it was in words and pictures, now it is no longer a living, breathing entity being added to one day at a time but history, receding inexorably, savagely into the past at a rate of one day per day.

Also in the Jewish tradition the Mourner's Kaddish is regarded as the definitive prayer for the dead. Its most distinctive feature is that it makes absolutely no reference to death, grief, mourning or bereavement at all; it is solely a hymn to and of praise to God, God's goodness praised *in spite of* loss. (If you want an actual Jewish prayer for the dead you have to look to something like *El Malei Rachamim*, for example, which *is* about bereavement, grief and remembrance). Nevertheless it has since time immemorial become known as a prayer of death, grief, bereavement and memorial. In the Jewish tradition to say kaddish (which isn't a solitary prayer but has to be said in the presence of a *minyan*; that's to say a quorum of ten Jewish males over the age of thirteen) for one's lost loved ones is to remember them, to memorialise them. Leon Wieselter's book *Kaddish* describes his own long and complex journey through his grief at the death of his father. Not a Jew, I cannot legitimately say kaddish for Rhona in the formal sense, though informally I say it every day of my life that passes in what I do, in what I say, in what I write and in what I remember. I am not a Jew. Jew-ish, perhaps, but not a Jew, and am therefore not permitted, at least by Orthodox authorities, to offer the usual prayers for Rhona to a Jewish God whose existence I at the very least doubt. Judaism does death at least as well as does Christianity and in many ways perhaps even better: Judaism is a life-orientated religion, concentrating on *olam ha-ze* (this world) much more than on *olam ha-ba* (the world to come). Though not generally regarded as big drinkers the traditional Jewish drinking toast is *l'chayim*, 'to life!'; but it recognises and realises the importance of death, bereavement and mourning as no other tradition I know, with some magnificent liturgy which rises to heights of beautiful if tragic poetry. *Kaddish, Yizkor, El Malei Rachamim*. It is customary on the anniversary of a death to light a *yahrzeit* candle which burns for twenty-four hours. When the day comes, and it is fast approaching, I shall do so.

This book is a memoir, not a self-help manual. There are plenty of those around (in my experience some excellent, some wretched and all points between). I've tried to give an honest and accurate account of the life that I shared with an entirely remarkable, utterly irreplaceable individual for a few weeks short of twenty-one years. I haven't sought to write a 'how-to' guide on navigating bereavement as I don't set myself up as (and quite rightly nobody would take me as) any kind of role model for the grieving. For a very long time after Rhona's death I gave up on food, on personal hygiene, started smoking again and took to the bottle — or rather many, many, many bottles — to an almost suicidal extent. I actively contemplated suicide. To the recently bereaved I can of course give the obvious counsels which are a matter of common sense; try to eat at least something nutritious and nourishing as little and as often as you can manage even when you feel that food is the very last thing you can face; if you can't sleep (and chances are you won't) at least try to get some decent rest; for the sake of your health do all that you can to resist the temptation (and you will be tempted) to numb yourself temporarily with alcohol and/or other drugs; take every offer of help from family and friends; consider bereavement counselling — help is out there; generally look after yourself even when, *especially* when, you don't want to be here any more; if you find yourself having suicidal thoughts seek professional help immediately, and so forth. But I haven't set out to write a handbook to grief. I'm not qualified and can't, don't and won't present myself as any kind of authority, or at any rate no more so than anybody else who has suffered a shattering loss. It takes a special kind of knowledge and expertise to dare to help people through the worst pain of their lives; Jonathan Santlofer wrote *The Widower's Notebook*, not *The Widower's Guidebook*. I can only tell our story and relate the facts and the feelings honestly as they actually occurred. Speaking from experience, the one and only thing I would strongly, in fact urgently recommend is not to the bereaved but to the not-yet bereaved: if there is someone in your life whom you love deeply and dearly, someone who is to you as Rhona was to me, every moment of every day take as many photographs and as much video footage of them as you possibly can — almost everyone carries a smartphone everywhere with them these days so it's not difficult to do. One day those images and that footage, along with your memories, may be all you have left.

Several times in the course of this account I have inevitably made reference to religious or spiritual beliefs; now I suppose that I have to turn to last things at the last. I have never been, am not and can never see myself being anywhere even slightly close to being a conventionally religious man; there was no point during Rhona's illness, not even in the last terrible hours in extremis in the ITU, when I could have prayed or bargained with God or the gods (*please … if Rhona survives I'll do/ won't do this, that or the other*) but didn't. Faith is presumably either there or it isn't; I've never been a fan of religion, allegedly 'organised' or not, and more often than not I've seen it as more of a curse to humanity than a blessing — as a dying Dennis Potter put it, more the wound than the bandage. I even have the modern non-believer's squint-eyed suspicion of terms such as 'spiritual', although perhaps inevitably I now find myself rather more open to such a dimension in life than ever before if interpreted with sufficient latitude. Like Cathy Rentzenbrink in *A Manual for Heartache* I don't necessarily rule anything out anymore. It can of course be charged that this is no more than foul-weather hope, disregarded in the good times and born solely of losing Rhona, and that's an entirely fair and just allegation. Of course it is. Nobody needs a life belt until they fall into the sea. If this is desperate hope born of terrible grief, so be it. But I don't entirely think so. I like to believe that I am sufficiently self-aware to know my own motives. I flatter myself that I'm open-minded and respectful of any beliefs that not merely bring solace and succour to the individual but those that respect what I regard as the best of human and humane values (with which many ostensibly religious values are in sharp disagreement, in my experience and opinion). I respect but can't share the faith of someone like, for example, the presenter Simon Thomas so movingly expressed in his beautiful though harrowing memoir *Love, Interrupted*. I remain an innately sceptical rationalist to the marrow of my bones. I don't know if there is a God or there are gods or not and if there is or are, what that God or those gods desire of us and if my life has been acceptable in His (Her? Its? Their?) sight. I haven't the faintest idea what it is like, what it *would* be like, actually to believe such things; to take them as actually, literally true, which I don't and never have. It may be that a capacity for belief of this kind, or rather the lack of such beliefs, is akin to being tone deaf or colour-blind; something that some people have and others do not. What, if anything at all, happens to personal consciousness after death I haven't the faintest idea (and I don't believe that anybody else does either, whatever they may claim). A great part of the Jewish tradition, the one with which I'm most familiar, is confessedly vague and widely averse to speculation on the existence and nature of an afterlife. As Rabbi Julia Neuberger puts it in *On Being Jewish*, many Jews are decidedly shaky when it comes to the idea of an afterlife since the Biblical texts that touch upon the subject are hardly a model of clarity; they are at best ambiguous and open to all sorts of interpretation. For those who truly and sincerely hold such beliefs about the fate of the individual after physical death there may be tremendous comfort and solace, but equally to me it seems that such beliefs raise just as many unanswerable and painful questions as they provide off-the-peg answers. I can't help but share the sentiments of Julian Barnes in *Levels of Life*:

> I do not believe I shall ever see her again. Never see, hear, touch, embrace, listen to, laugh with; never again wait for her footstep, smile at the sound of an opening door, fit her body into mine, mine into hers. Nor do I believe we shall meet again in some dematerialised form. I believe dead is dead.

And yet, like a tongue continually probing an aching tooth, we speculate anyway, over and over and over again. I've read my Bertrand Russell and other great philosophers and am minimally philosophically savvy enough to know that whatever I believe could be wrong. It may be that the need to believe, the *hope* that those we have lost are still aware in some sense and perhaps even capable of being aware of the living and their actions, is almost as old as the human species itself. With Mencken I have learnt in the hardest way possible that sometimes the temptation to believe — to want to believe — that some essence, some kernel of all that was my Rhona persists somehow, somewhere, in some form is irresistible. For the first time in my life I am envious of those like Simon Thomas who as a Christian sincerely — although at times shakily — believes that the death of his wife Gemma (herself also a Christian) is a temporary interruption in an ongoing love story which will continue after his own death. I am not a man of faith, but in the words of Ann Thorp's poem 'Belief':

> I have to believe
> That you still exist
> Somewhere,
> That you still watch me
> Sometimes,
> That you still love me
> Somehow.
>
> I have to believe
> That life has meaning
> Somehow,
> That I am useful here
> Sometimes,
> That I make small differences
> Sometimes.
>
> I have to believe
> That I need to stay here
> For some time,
> That all this teaches me
> Something,
> So that I can meet you again
> Somewhere.

That may be the case or it may not. We can only be as content as we are able to be to wait and see, with as much optimistic hope and faith as our nature allows us to have, if there is anything at all to wait and see. In my case that's not much. It's not necessarily wholly absent but it's a poor, frail thing. I have faced — and at least so far survived — the worst possible, impossible, imaginable, unimaginable loss; it has made the end of my own life, whenever and however it may come, more tolerable and frankly at times downright welcome. I was holding

Rhona's hand when her eyes closed on this world for the last time. One day it will be my own turn. I don't know if anybody will be holding my hand when the moment comes and am not particularly bothered. I don't know what, if anything, ensues. It is a fairly shop-worn commonplace to say that one fears the process of dying more than the state of being dead itself — whatever that may entail, whether something or nothing — but having seen what life can do (that is to say, what the death of others can do to your life) my own demise holds absolutely no fears for me. It didn't before; it most definitely doesn't now. I am afraid of life, a Rhona-less life, not death. I can't currently find a source for the story and I hope that it isn't a false memory, but I can distinctly recall reading, many years ago, about the writer Roald Dahl who tragically lost his daughter Olivia to measles aged only seven. (Dahl understandably became a fierce and passionate advocate of vaccination thereafter). Decades later, when Dahl as an old man was himself dying of cancer, he is said to have remarked that if his daughter could die, so could he. And he of course duly did. I have something of the same feeling with Rhona. I am a quite monumental physical coward to the marrow of my bones, never more so than when it comes to medical things, hospitals and physical pain and anything associated with illness. There is absolutely no way in the world that I could ever manifest the sheer bloody-minded courage that Rhona demonstrated in her final years; handfuls of pills and vodka, a firearm if I could get one or the noose are to me infinitely preferable to the long, lingering, lost hours in our super-modern, gleaming, ultra high-tech cathedrals of sickness and death. I am not remotely afraid of the death that I've actively courted at various stretches of my life, some of them quite lengthy; I've no great interest in what happens to me and am far, far more afraid of what will become of the remaining artefacts which are now the only physical, visible, tangible relics of a long life together. In the middle of sleepless nights I worry not about my own mortality but about Rhona's clothes and our kitchen utensils and multiple other mundane things and what will happen to them, not about myself. I don't matter; Rhona's favourite anorak, our best bread knife, the blender that used to live on top of the fridge — these are the things that matter, because they're all that's left that Rhona looked at, touched, chose, wanted.

To be bereaved in any sense is to be altered profoundly and permanently; some no doubt may find for the better in certain respects but in my experience I can only say that it's for the worse. While I would imagine (and I can only imagine) that the death of a child may be the very worst possible type of loss, I don't want, mean or intend to construct a league table, a sliding scale of whose suffering is greater than somebody else's. It's not a competition. Grief is grief whoever you may grieve for. To lose the person you love most in the world is to be changed against your will for ever.

It is part of received wisdom these days — to a certain extent it has always been — that a 'successful' life, amongst other things, is one lived without regrets; the *My Way* approach. While superficially attractive, after a moment's serious critical thought this sounds to me like the life advice of the sociopath. As Rust Cohle observes in the first series of *True Detective*: "People without a conscience usually do have a good time." Regrets multiply the more one dwells upon the past. Not merely "The good not done,/The love not given,/Time torn off unused" as Philip Larkin put it; these are negatives, sins of omission. While it is proverbial that we regret the things we didn't do rather than the things we did — the Henry James way: "Live, live all you can. It's a terrible mistake not to" —, that doesn't apply in every case. When there is regret for what one *did* do, regret bites hard indeed. Religious people talk about a reckoning, a final judgement with their God, but in my fantasies there is only a reckoning and a final judgement with Rhona. It may be that in some way we had that while she was still alive but (as it turned out) dying by degrees. If that is so — *if* that is so, which I don't know — then perhaps the last judgement was: you did me wrong, very, very wrong, but I forgive you. Now try to forgive yourself.

I struggle with this still every day. Struggle badly. Chronic remorse, as Aldous Huxley wrote at the beginning of *Brave New World*, is a most undesirable sentiment; repent, make what amends you can and move on with the resolve to behave better in future. Rolling in the muck is no way to get clean. Maybe in caring for her I did go some way towards making amends to Rhona, yet I still wrestle, still brood over my heinous wrongdoing. Maybe I always will; I don't think that there will ever be a time when I'm not haunted to some extent by the shame, guilt and remorse of having overlooked Rhona to such an extent that I had an affair, however brief it may have been. As Simone de Beauvoir wrote in *A Very Easy Death*:

> When someone you love dies you pay for the sin of outliving her with a thousand piercing regrets. Her death brings to light her unique quality; she grows as vast as the world that her absence annihilates for her and whose whole existence was caused by her being there; you feel that she should have had more room in your life — all the room, if need be [...] But since you never do all you might for someone — not even within the arguable limits that you have set yourself — you have plenty of room left for self-reproach.

I'm inclined to agree; plenty of room indeed. And *pace* Huxley, perhaps a fairly regular reminder of the pain I inflicted on Rhona by my thoughtless and selfish betrayal is not necessarily a wholly bad thing.

The other side of the coin is that, however guilty and ashamed I have felt, still feel and will always feel about betraying Rhona by having an affair I feel no guilt — desperate, scalding sorrow, yes, but no guilt — and also immense pride about the fact that I was able to love her and care for her to the utmost of my abilities in her final three and a half years in particular. I was devastated to have found out, not just once but twice, that I was unable to be a living kidney donor but sufficiently self-aware to realise that this wasn't my fault; my kidneys simply were how they were and there was nothing I could do to change that. When my mum died in 2001 one of the greatest consolations was that she died knowing how much she was loved by me and that nothing of any great import or significance was left unsaid; no loose ends, no unfinished business. To a large degree — not entirely; perhaps that's impossible in all human relationships since there's always one more loving word to have spoken, one more loving gesture to have performed; but mostly — I believe that the same obtains with Rhona. Whatever foolish, stupid, selfish mistakes I made, and goodness only knows I made plenty large and small, I have to believe that she knew I worshipped the ground she walked on and would have bottled the air that she breathed and that I had come back to Blaby after our four-month separation and that I stayed there because I wanted to be with her at the time, all the time, in her too-short life when she needed me most and because I loved her beyond any power of mine to describe. I am about as pleased with the books I've written as I know how to be; I'm too insecure and too self-critical to think of any of them as more than just about all right, occasionally. I'm delighted to have looked after the animals I've known in my life. But I can honestly say that I have done one unalloyed and unambiguously good, selfless and altruistic thing with my existence and that was to care for Rhona when she needed care the most. The fact that she became ill was our tragedy; that I was able to look after her was and is my privilege. As an epigraph for *Paperwork* I chose a few lines from Donald Hall's poem 'Ardor': "Her death was the worst thing/that could happen/and caring for her was best." I can't improve on that.

Rhona was ill for a comparatively long time — almost three and a half years — but at the very end died suddenly. Shockingly, bewilderingly suddenly, which amongst other reasons may explain why I 'handled' her death so badly. She died with the first few Christmas presents that I'd already bought for her tucked away in the usual hidey-holes in the loft awaiting wrapping paper and sticky tape, exactly the same as every other year. True, her death didn't come for example with the abrupt brutality of death in a random road traffic accident — it's a mathematical certainty that today there will be people who eat breakfast, kiss their spouses and children, head off out in the car and never come home again. But as poorly as she was, in Rhona's case it was three days and a handful of hours in hospital and then the end. While it's true that nobody can survive on haemodialysis for ever, no death sentence was handed down. Treatment — cure, ideally — was being actively pursued. Rhona was on the transplant list for a donated kidney. She was earmarked for aortic valve replacement surgery. Rhona was not told that she was going to die and did not expect to. Neither did anyone else. There was no anticipatory grief, or at least not over a time scale of longer than a handful of hours. There was none of the protracted expectation of death that comes with the diagnosis of a terminal condition such as an inoperable cancer or motor neurone disease, for example. There was none of the agonising attrition, the gradual loss of personality, the death-in-life of Alzheimer's disease or any other form of dementia. How people react in the face of such diagnoses — how *I* would have reacted had one been delivered — I have absolutely no idea. There will come a day when I too must face my own end; whether it comes soon or late, whether it comes abruptly and without warning or is a drawn-out process due to a lingering illness I can't say. Those things are not within my ken. But whatever may be the case I have specifically requested that my ashes be deposited at Weston Road cemetery in Stevenage where Rhona was laid to rest with John. My connection to Stevenage stands and falls entirely on Rhona; and whereas once I wanted to have my ashes buried in my home county of Leicestershire, this time P.R. (post-Rhona) has made me see things differently. While Rhona was alive I always used to think, hope and expect that I would be buried in Leicestershire and made certain directions to that effect. Not any more. Weston Road it has to be. I understand and honour Rhona's decision to be buried in Stevenage, though as a non-driver the fact that that cemetery is eighty miles away and difficult to get to by road or rail is a source of sorrow to me. I can't easily visit her grave; I can't just pop round when I feel like it as the more fortunate (for want of a far better word ...) amongst the bereaved are sometimes able to. Logistically and financially it has to be planned well in advance like a military exercise and that saddens me, I have to say. But we can at least share more or less the same area of land in death as we did in so much of our life. Caring for Rhona, across the whole of our twenty-one years together but especially the last three and a half years, was an act of love; after concluding this memoir joining her in death at Weston Road must stand as the last act of love I'm able to perform for the beautiful woman with whom I shared my days — seven thousand six hundred and twenty-seven days to be exact, if you count from New Year's Eve 1997 to the day of Rhona's death. (No, I'm not that good at maths and yes, there are websites that can calculate this sort of thing for you).

I write nearly ten months after Rhona's death. Sometimes, bizarrely, it feels like yesterday. At other times, equally bizarrely, it feels like ten thousand years ago. More bizarrely than either sometimes it feels like both simultaneously. I live still with my aunt Joan, now ninety-one, and the cats, now down to four. I eat too little and drink vastly too much; about the former I am unconcerned and of the latter I enjoy it too much to think of reining it in. I try to maintain an interest in cooking, even if largely vicariously with hefty cookery books and TV programmes. I sometimes walk though not often, not nearly as often as this quondam champion walker used to. I buy books as assiduously as I ever did but don't read very much now. Concentration has dwindled and in any case there doesn't seem to be much point. I have now been down to Stevenage to visit the grave twice, once with my aunt, once alone. As difficult as it is I intend to continue to do so as often as I'm able. I look at the multiple photographs taken of our shared life, glad that I took as many as I did, grieved that I didn't take so many more. More than any of these things, mostly I think and write about Rhona and our life together. I scribble letters to Rhona in my diary most days and imagine that I'm still talking to her. In addition to my diary, soon to reach its thirty-sixth birthday, I have spent the past several months working on two books about her: *Paperwork*, a collection of verses to, for and about her, published a month ago at time of writing, and this memoir. When this is finished what the future may hold — what I am to do, where I am to go — I have absolutely no idea and actually no overwhelming interest in particular. I am not able to say that, all these months on, the pain is softening and the blow notably less than when it landed. That may change, although knowing myself as well as I do — perhaps too well for comfort — it seems unlikely. If I am honest I cannot say that potentially another thirty or even forty years of Rhona-less life holds any appeal for me. "Here is one of the worst things about having someone you love die," wrote Anna Quindlen in *Every Last One*: "It happens again every single morning." Every day is still another blow upon the bruise. Perhaps this is self-inflicted to a degree: all these months on I am still using our kitchen utensils, still eating long-lived food toted over from Blaby, still sleeping on pillows and pillowcases that Rhona slept on, still wearing clothing that Rhona and I bought. So be it. *Ich kann nicht anders*, as Martin Luther wrote in an entirely different context; I can't do otherwise. If I am to survive grief, mourning, bereavement, there will come the significant dates, the anniversaries, the holidays. In another couple of months' time I will — if I survive — be in a position to say "My wife died a year ago today". And then — if I survive — "My wife died two years ago today". And then — if I survive —: "My wife died three years ago today". And then — if I survive —: "Had she lived my wife would have been seventy today". If I survive, if I have a future that should have belonged with Rhona, to *us*, to a *we* and not only to a *me*, my own birthdays will accumulate. At forty-seven, fifty is the next big one, if I get there and don't have another, more serious heart attack in the meantime. Then fifty-five; sixty; sixty-seven, the age at which Rhona died; unthinkable to me now but forty-seven was doubtless unthinkable to my twenty year-old self. And no Rhona with which to share them. No Rhona with which to share anything anymore, come to that. Rhona sometimes used to say to me that, meeting me as she did when I was only twenty-five, she had had the best years of my life. Truer word was never spoken. While she (to my life-long shame, remorse and regret) unquestionably had some of the worst of me, I like to think, *I hope*, that she also had — such as it is — all of the best of me.

I was twenty-five when we met and forty-six when she died, the same age as Rhona was when we met. That's a hefty chunk of an important period of anybody's life and Rhona had it. For all its lows as well as highs, the downs as well as the ups — what else can you expect for two people together almost all the time for twenty-one years? — what Rhona and I had, what we created, was a *life*. And she was, whatever anybody else says or thinks, despite my grievous mistakes, the centre of mine. There are no perfect people in this world but sometimes — just sometimes — two people can be perfect for each other. To quote Julian Barnes yet again from *Levels of Life*:

> You put together two people [...] and sometimes the world is changed [...] sometimes, something new is made, and then the world is changed. Together [...] they are greater than their two separate selves. Together, they see further, and they see more clearly.

Together Rhona and I were greater than our two separate selves; we saw further and more clearly. We had a vision of a life together and we, perhaps without even knowing it or realising it at the time, pursued it and created it, created a *modus vivendi* that suited us both just about perfectly. Love, as Antoine de Saint-Exupéry famously wrote, does not consist in gazing at each other but in looking outward together in the same direction. For close to twenty-one years Rhona and I did just that: looked outward together in the same direction. For all our differences in trivial, footling things, even without explicitly articulating it, we had the same vision, the same concept of the kind of life we wanted to lead, the kind of home we wanted to live in, the kind of relationship — marriage, in essence — that we wanted to have. This is why I'm not remotely abashed to say that I believe, firmly and without hesitation or qualification, in the existence of soulmates; not, I hasten to add, in some kind of New Agey, foreordained, written-in-the-stars way — life is too ruled by sheer random chance for anything like that — but in the way that two total strangers can be thrown together by an accidental confluence of events and, however unlikely they may look to those on the outside, still find themselves a perfect match for each other, on the same wavelength and (as Rhona often used to say) filling in each other's gaps.

Now, however long I may live, I can only live day by day on the memories of my life with Rhona. Some captured in physical form — virtual form now — in photographs — we were together so long that we started off taking photographs with a camera into which one put an actual roll of film and then had developed, which these days seems impossibly quaint; in multiple albums and in video clips (too few of these), my diaries, emails, text messages; but all residing ultimately in my mind. Literally: in *The Long Goodbye* Meghan O'Rourke refers to a psychiatrist who said that "the people we most love do become a physical part of us, ingrained in our synapses, in the pathways where memories are created." If that is so, Rhona is within me in the most literal sense and always will be, laid down in my synapses, entwined in the wiring of my brain as long as it may persist. No day goes by, scarcely an hour come to that, sleeping or waking, in which some sight, sound, scent, taste, object, TV programme, doesn't remind me of her and evoke memories of our twenty-one years together. Like so many of the bereaved I talk to her more or less constantly, in my head at least. Some do it out loud, as I have done at times. Some no doubt think this madness. I think I don't care. Like H. L. Mencken I can never see anything — a particular TV programme, a particular book, a newspaper or magazine article, even a certain item of food — without the awakening of the desire to share it with her, immediately followed by the only too familiar stab of loss and emptiness. I can't see an item of clothing without mentally noting whether she who so loved to dress me up would approve or give it the thumbs down. My near-daily diary is in the form of letters addressed to her, a practice which started within days of her death. If this is unhealthy clinging bordering on complicated grief, so be it. It's not as though I'm bothered. *Ich kann nicht anders*, again. The pain is horrific but — while admitting that there is an undoubted element of masochism at play — as Julian Barnes has observed, pain is proof of love. Pain means not forgetting. In whatever life is left to me there will be no time in which I do not turn to one side or the other and think that I'm sharing with Wowo something I've heard — a stupid, probably (knowing me) off-colour joke; a comment; an item of news and current affairs; a passage in a book or magazine or newspaper; anything of interest — and not find her there. As the old saying has it, what can't be cured must be endured, and life now is a matter of endurance rather than living. I don't, can't, won't accept the situation; I can only put up with it for as long as I'm able, in a world which is no longer, can never again be that same world I shared with her for twenty-one magical, wonderful, painful, beautiful, tragic, joyous years.

Also in *The Long Goodbye* O'Rourke quotes (unattributed, but it's actually by Katherine Frank in the prologue to *Lucie Duff Gordon: A Passage to Egypt*, her biography of the Victorian author and translator) a profound passage about time and memory whose metaphor resonated strongly with me the first time I read it and haunts me still:

> We usually think of time as a river, a river like the Nile, with a strong, swift current bearing us further and further away from what we have been and towards the time when we will be not at all—birth, death and the brief transit of life in between. But perhaps we should think of time as a deep, still pool rather than a fast-flowing river. If time were a pool, we could kneel at its edge and gaze at our reflections and then beyond them to what lay deeper still. Instead of looking back at time, we could look down into it … and now and again different features of the past—different sights and sounds and voices and dreams—would rise to the surface; rise and subside, and the deep pool would hold them all, so that nothing was lost and nothing ever went away.

Nothing was lost and nothing ever went away. If only, if only, if only. If two people love each other, Hemingway wrote, there can be no happy end to it. Julian Barnes said more or less exactly the same thing when he writes that every love story is a potential grief story. Once love — true, genuine, committed love — enters the picture there will be heartbreak somewhere along the line sooner or later. There will always be separation, willed or not. Such is the human condition. And yet for all this bleak counsel we do it still. Some people may do it repeatedly, forgetting, as with women having more than one child, the discomfort of pregnancy and the pain of birth the first time round — because we hope, and some of us discover, that the rewards outbalance the sorrow. We constantly aspire to love, as Barnes puts it, because love is the meeting point of truth and magic.

I began this account with an ending; I end it now with the beginning. Once upon a time there was a young man who met a much older woman — thrown together by random chance, fortune, fate, the hand of God, Cupid's arrow, whatever may be your preferred explanation — and the two fell in love. They loved, quarrelled, made love, quarrelled again, were incredibly happy, were desperately sad, were furiously angry, were tenderly loving, at one point parted but soon came back together. In due course the woman, unfortunately, became ill and died, and the man who cared for her, equally unfortunately, had to survive a little longer without her. They lived together long and, despite the downs as well as the ups, largely happily, but not ever after. Nobody does. I was, and am, an exceedingly ordinary man who met someone utterly extraordinary and to whom something extraordinary happened.

I have no future, but that is perfectly all right. "Don't look backwards; you're not going that way" is one of those innumerable twee quotes that crops up online now and again. But that's exactly where I'm going; back to the past even as the clocks ticks into the future. I have no need or desire to look forward, for I can turn around and see my past, *our* past, our twenty-one years together, spread out before me like a landscape. In *Dying: A Memoir* the Australian writer Cory Taylor, dying of melanoma, wrote that she had no use for a bucket list; she was too caught up in her past life, in the things she actually *had* done, than to waste time on those things that she hadn't. I remember Rhona in just about every single last thing that I do and everywhere I go. Most of the time I cry, sometimes I smile, sometimes I laugh, which is much as you'd expect for two people who were together so much for so long.

Perhaps when our time comes, as for each and every one of us it one day must, something beautiful beyond the comprehension of our finite human minds lies in store for us.

On the other hand perhaps at the end of our lives in this world an endless dreamless sleep awaits us all.

It strikes me as a win-win situation whatever the truth of it may be. In either case it will be peaceful, and above all else I shall join my Rhona in it.

Although I can't say that I believe in or share his rock-solid faith that he and his wife would be reunited, in the words of Bishop Henry King, from 'The Exequy':

Sleep on, my Love, in thy cold bed
Never to be disquieted!
My last good-night! Thou wilt not wake
Till I thy fate shall overtake:
Till age, or grief, or sickness, must
Marry my body to that dust
It so much loves; and fill the room
My heart keeps empty in thy tomb.
Stay for me there: I will not fail
To meet thee in that hollow vale.
And think not much of my delay:
I am already on the way,
And follow thee with all the speed
Desire can make, or sorrows breed.
Each minute is a short degree
And every hour a step towards thee …

Perhaps King was right and his faith not misplaced. If every hour is a step away from the living Rhona — which is certainly how it feels — every hour might, for all I know, be a step closer. Who knows? I don't know and know that I don't know, and know that I don't know that I don't know. I am already on the way in either case.

You were my life. I love you and miss you more than I'm able to say, Wo. And always will.

Steven Payne
September 2019

Appendix

The Exequy

Accept, thou shrine of my dead saint,
Instead of dirges this complaint;
And for sweet flowers to crown thy herse
Receive a strew of weeping verse
From thy grieved friend whom thou might'st see
Quite melted into tears for thee.
Dear loss! Since thy untimely fate,
My task hath been to meditate
On thee, on thee! Thou art the book,
The library whereon I look,
Tho' almost blind. For thee, loved clay,
I languish out, not live, the day ...
Thou hast benighted me; thy set
This eve of blackness did beget,
Who wast my day (tho' overcast
Before thou hadst thy noontime past):
And I remember must in tears
Thou scarce hadst seen so many years
As day tells hours. By thy clear sun
My love and fortune first did run;

But thou wilt never more appear
Folded within my hemisphere,
Since both thy light and motion,
Like a fled star, is fall'n and gone,
And 'twixt me and my soul's dear wish
The earth now interposed is ...
I could allow thee for a time
To darken me and my sad clime;
Were it a month, a year, or ten,
I would thy exile live till then,
And all that space my mirth adjourn—
So thou wouldst promise to return,
And putting off thy ashy shroud
At length disperse this sorrow's cloud.
But woe is me! the longest date
Too narrow is to calculate
These empty hopes: never shall I
Be so much blest as to descry
A glimpse of thee, till that day come
Which shall the earth to cinders doom,
And a fierce fever must calcine
The body of this world—like thine,
My little world! That fit of fire
Once off, our bodies shall aspire
To our souls' bliss: then we shall rise
And view ourselves with clearer eyes
In that calm region where no night
Can hide us from each other's sight.
Meantime thou hast her, earth: much good
May my harm do thee! Since it stood
With Heaven's will I might not call
Her longer mine, I give thee all
My short-lived right and interest
In her whom living I loved best.
Be kind to her, and prithee look

Thou write into thy Doomsday book
Each parcel of this rarity
Which in thy casket shrined doth lie,
As thou wilt answer Him that lent
—Not gave—thee my dear monument.
So close the ground, and 'bout her shade
Black curtains draw: my bride is laid.
Sleep on, my Love, in thy cold bed
Never to be disquieted!
My last good-night! Thou wilt not wake
Till I thy fate shall overtake:
Till age, or grief, or sickness, must
Marry my body to that dust
It so much loves; and fill the room
My heart keeps empty in thy tomb.
Stay for me there: I will not fail
To meet thee in that hollow vale.
And think not much of my delay:
I am already on the way,
And follow thee with all the speed
Desire can make, or sorrows breed.
Each minute is a short degree
And every hour a step towards thee …
At night when I betake to rest,
Next morn I rise nearer my west
Of life, almost by eight hours' sail
Than when sleep breath'd his drowsy gale.
Thus from the sun my bottom steers,
And my day's compass downwards bears;
Nor labour I to stem the tide
Through which to thee I swiftly glide
'Tis true—with shame and grief I yield—
Thou, like the van, first took'st in the field;
And gotten hast the victory
In thus adventuring to die

Before me, whose more years might crave
A just precedence in the grave.
But hark! My pulse, like a soft drum,
Beats my approach, tells thee I come;
And slow howe'er my marches be
I shall at last sit down by thee.
The thought of this bids me go on
And wait my dissolution
With hope and comfort. Dear—forgive
The crime—I am content to live
Divided, with but half a heart,
Till we shall meet and never part.

Bishop Henry King (1592-1669)

Acknowledgements

There are so many people who deserve so much gratitude that it's hard to know even where to begin and, what's worse, the fear is of leaving someone out.

Rhona's family, obviously. All of Rhona's friends, some going all the way back to their schooldays in the 1950s and 60s. In fact, everyone who loved Rhona at any stage of her life but especially those who offered practical, emotional and moral support in her final illnesses and after her death.

In my case specifically, the best friends that anybody could ever hope to have in their lives, Adam Fox and Vicky Wheeler, who offered unstinting support to a shattered, utterly bereft, frequently monumentally drunk and often weeping man at all hours of the day and night.

The bereavement counsellors that I saw, especially N. whose listening ear and patient support over many months has been little short of remarkable.

The assorted medical staff at all three of the University Hospitals of Leicester; the Leicester Royal Infirmary, Leicester General Hospital and Glenfield Hospital, as well as The Spire hospital in Oadby, Hazelmere surgery in Blaby and Lavender Road dental practice, Leicester. There were so many of these across so many departments and disciplines in three different hospitals (as well as the other places mentioned) that it would be impossible to name every person even slightly associated with Rhona's care in the final three and a half years of her life; this acknowledgement must stand as a profound, heartfelt collective thank you to each and every last one of them.

My solicitor Noel McNicholas, whose expertise, calmness, wise counsel, steady hand on the tiller in turbulent times and patience with a distraught client were more of a comfort and encouragement than I know how to express.

In loving memory of Leslie Arnold Goldstone — Rhona's dad — who passed away suddenly but peacefully at a ripe age in 2010 and who, thank goodness, never had to see his daughter in illness.

Needless to say — the phrase that people always use when they go ahead and say it anyway — the greatest thanks (as though the feeble word 'thanks' can ever do it justice) go to the one person who need not be named and cannot now be thanked.

Bibliography

Many of these books are referred to in the main body of this account. This bibliography in no way pretends to be an exhaustive list of mis. lit. — such a catalogue would practically make an entire book in its own right — and I certainly didn't read in any kind of systematic way at all; it's no more than an individual choice of some of those books which I found most useful ('enjoyable' is in the circumstances scarcely the right word …) in the aftermath of Rhona's death, of which I read so many (once I was able to concentrate long enough to be able to read anything of any length again) that I fancy myself almost as something of an expert. It's a bit of a mish-mash (a Yiddish phrase, incidentally, and pronounced *mish-mosh*); some of the books listed here are self-help books; some memoirs; some poetry. There is a lot of highly personal and incredibly painful reading here that the recently bereaved in particular could find very hard to take and I wouldn't encourage anybody not already so inclined to undertake a course of grief-reading if they don't feel up to it, but there's also much candour, strength and wisdom. These are deeply sad books about the saddest thing in the world but they need not be depressing.

At time of writing most of these books are, to the best of my knowledge, currently in print but those which may have gone out of print can be acquired by the usual methods.

Abse, Dannie: *The Presence* — Both doctor and poet, *The Presence* is the diary kept by Abse following the death of his wife Joan in June 2005 in the car accident in which he himself was injured.

Aitkenhead, Decca: *All At Sea* — The *Guardian* journalist's partner Tony drowned on holiday in Jamaica while saving one of the couple's sons from the same fate. *All At Sea* is Aitkenhead's account of their unusual but solid relationship and how she managed to survive bereavement.

Bennett, Paul: *Loving Grief* — A short but eloquent meditation (with a pleasing double meaning to its title) on bereavement following the death of Paul Bennett's wife Bonnie from a brain tumour.

Brazier, Jeff: *The Grief Survival Guide: How to Navigate Loss and All That Comes With It* — A hefty and detailed guide to 'doing' grief healthily by the former partner of reality TV personality Jade Goody, who died of cancer in 2009 aged just twenty-seven.

Brownlee, Lucie: *Life After You* — Lucie Brownlee's husband Mark died very suddenly of a dissected aorta at thirty-seven, leaving behind not only a desperately grieving widow but an infant daughter. *Life After You* (originally published as *Me After You*) is Lucie's account of her journey through bereavement.

Coles, Rev. Richard: *The Madness of Grief: A Memoir of Love and Loss* — A beautifully written account of the loss of Rev. Coles's husband David (himself an Anglican vicar).

Collick, Elizabeth: *Through Grief: The Bereavement Journey* — A short but engaging and wise volume.

Devine, Megan: *It's OK That You're Not OK: Meeting Grief and Loss in a Culture That Doesn't Understand* — In 2009 Megan Devine saw her partner Matt accidentally drown before her eyes; her book is a lengthy and compassionate — although brutal — account of how it's OK not to be OK even when, or especially when, others expect you to be.

Didion, Joan: *The Year of Magical Thinking* — One of the more famous grief memoirs, Joan Didion's husband, fellow writer John Gregory Dunne, died suddenly of a massive heart attack days after their daughter Quintana was rushed to hospital suffering from pneumonia and septic shock. *The Year of Magical Thinking* is Didion's account of this double tragedy.

Dunn, Douglas: *Elegies* — A heart-breaking collection of poems about the final illness and death of the poet's wife Leslie in 1981.

Faber, Michel: *Undying* — A truly beautiful volume of poetry about the novelist and poet's late wife Eva.

Ferdinand, Rio: *Thinking Out Loud* — In 2015 the former England footballer lost his wife Rebecca to breast cancer at the age of just thirty-four, leaving behind not only a grieving widower but three young children, and would go on to lose his mother to bladder cancer just two years afterwards. *Thinking Out Loud* is a raw and highly personal account of the aftermath of that double tragedy and how a still young and recently widowed celebrity father coped with bereavement.

Hall, Donald: *The Best Day, the Worst Day: Life with Jane Kenyon* — A prose work, this is Hall's account of the illness (leukaemia), death and aftermath of the death of his wife, the fellow poet Jane Kenyon.

Hall, Donald: *The Painted Bed* — To my mind a companion piece to *Without*, Hall continues the themes of his life with Jane Kenyon, nursing her until her death and the effects of bereavement.

Hall, Donald: *Without* — Arguably the best-known and potentially the best-regarded of Hall's many volumes of poetry, *Without* chronicles the dying and death of his wife Jane Kenyon from leukaemia.

Holland, Debra: *The Essential Guide to Grief and Grieving* — A comprehensive manual for negotiating various kinds of grief, including the loss of a child, of a friendship, a marriage, of a job, of pets.

Ironside, Virginia: *You'll Get Over It: The Rage of Bereavement* — One of the very earliest books I read in the wake of the loss of Rhona (ordered on the same day that she died in fact), still one of the best and in many ways one of the most shocking in its raw and at times brutal honesty. No punches are pulled here about the horrific nature of grief and the fact that life can never be the same again — even that some people may never truly find themselves 'recovered' from bereavement. A sometimes difficult, sometimes uncomfortable book, but one of the most truthful about the realities of grief.

Jamison, Kay Redfield: *Nothing Was the Same* — Jamison, a distinguished professor of psychiatry and herself a life-long sufferer of bipolar disorder, was married to Richard Wyatt, also a psychiatrist specialising in the study and treatment of schizophrenia. He died of cancer aged 63 in 2002; the marriage, his illness, death and its aftermath are recounted in this beautifully written memoir.

Kessler, David and Kübler-Ross, Elisabeth: *On Grief and Grieving* — Superior (in my opinion at any rate) to Kübler-Ross's better-known 1969 book *On Death and Dying*, this book applies Kübler-Ross's famous stages of grief model to the bereaved in a way never intended in the earlier work.

Lewis, C. S.: *A Grief Observed* — Potentially the most famous bereavement memoir of them all, *A Grief Observed* was born out of the notebooks kept by Lewis in the aftermath of the death from cancer of his American wife Joy after just four years of marriage. Lewis himself survived Joy by only three years. As is well known Lewis was, amongst other things, a popular theologian and the overt Christian theme of the book, the questioning of God and of faith, won't be to everybody's taste — it's not to mine — but it can be glossed over in favour of the wise insights which are not faith-dependent.

McCormack, Jerusha: *Grieving: A Beginner's Guide* — A wise and compassionate guide through the grieving process, as much as the subtitle is superfluous: in grief everyone is a beginner at least at some point.

Mead, Geoff: *Gone in the Morning: A Writer's Journey of Bereavement* — A former senior policeman-turned-writer and storyteller, Geoff Mead's wife Chris died little more than a year after being diagnosed with an aggressive and inoperable brain tumour. *Gone in the Morning* — the title comes from a poem written by Chris — is a loving memorial to a tender love story.

Morris, Sue: *Overcoming Grief* — Written by a clinical psychologist, the book concentrates on using the techniques of cognitive behavioural therapy for managing grief.

Murphy, Sylvia: *Surviving Your Partner* — A short but easy-to read book offering a wealth of hands-on practical advice (dealing with finances and so forth) for those who have lost a life partner.

Oates, Joyce Carol: *A Widow's Story: A Memoir* — A novelist's lengthy and frequently harrowing account of the sudden death of her husband from a hospital-acquired infection following a bout of pneumonia and the subsequent tormented journey through at times suicidal widowhood.

O'Rourke, Meghan: *The Long Goodbye*: Poet, critic and editor, Meghan O'Rourke's mother Barbara died of bowel cancer aged fifty-five. This deeply affecting memoir details O'Rourke's reaction to that death and the grief that ensued.

Parkes, Colin Murray and Prigerson, Holly G.: *Bereavement: Studies of Grief in Adult Life* — A classic work, now in its fourth edition, by possibly the world's leading expert on bereavement and grief, Colin Murray Parkes. Dense but readable.

Paxman, Maddy: *The Great Below: A Journey Into Loss* — Maddy Paxman's husband was the fine poet Michael Donaghy who in 2004 died of a brain haemorrhage aged fifty. *The Great Below* is as the subtitle states an account of Maddy's journey through unexpected death, bereavement and suddenly finding herself a single parent.

Reid, Christopher: *A Scattering* — A collection of poems about the poet's wife, Lucinda, and her death from cancer and his grief afterwards.

Rentzenbrink, Cathy: *A Manual for Heartache* — In 1990, aged just sixteen, Cathy Rentzenbrink's beloved brother Matty was struck by a hit-and-run driver and received massive head injuries; he spent the next eight years in a persistent vegetative state until treatment was withdrawn and he died, a tragedy related in her first book *The Last Act of Love* (a sad but beautiful book also well worth reading, by the way). *A Manual for Heartache* can be thought of as a more general companion volume to the earlier book.

Roe, Gary: *Heartbroken: Healing from the Loss of a Spouse* — An approachable, easy-to-read book in bite-sized chunks about coping with the death of a life partner.

Samuel, Julia: *Grief Works*: A remarkable book by a specialist grief counsellor, divided into sections addressing specific forms of loss (death of a partner/parent/sibling/child, etc.).

Santlofer, Jonathan: *The Widower's Notebook: A Memoir* — A profoundly moving, sometimes darkly funny, beautifully written meditation on widowerhood following the sudden (and unexplained) death of Santlofer's wife Joy. It would perhaps be unfair of me to pick specific favourites amongst all the grief memoirs and other books I read, but Santlofer is particularly good on how society deals with bereaved men and women differently.

Taylor, Liz: *Living With Loss: A Guide for the Recently Widowed* — Sound, practical advice from a wise guide.

Thomas, Simon: *Love, Interrupted* — Gemma, the wife of TV presenter Simon Thomas, died of acute myeloid leukaemia at the age of forty just three days after being diagnosed. Thomas's memoir describes his devastation, suddenly becoming the single parent of a young child, his descent into alcoholism and ultimately his survival.

Wallbank, Susan: *The Empty Bed: Bereavement and the Loss of Love* — A sensitively-handled book about bereavement — obviously — and issues that many find difficult, such as sexuality after bereavement and meeting a new partner.

Want, Barbara: *Why Not Me? A Story of Love and Loss* — Barbara Want's husband, the respected journalist and broadcaster Nick Clarke, died of cancer; a broadcaster herself, *Why Not Me?* is Barbara's moving account of his diagnosis, his terminal illness, his death and its aftermath and coping not only with her grief but two young sons.

Wolfelt, Alan D.: *Healing a Spouse's Grieving Heart: 100 Practical Ideas After Your Husband or Wife Dies* — Exactly as the title states, a hundred hands-on suggestions on how to navigate the white water of grief after losing a spouse.

Wolfelt, Alan D.: *When Your Soulmate Dies* — A well-written, highly emotional book about surviving the loss of one's soulmate.

Useful organisations

Many of the following organisations (some specific to my and Rhona's story, as will be obvious) are registered charities who get no government funding and rely on charitable donations. All welcome donations — of money; of goods; of time — no matter how small.

Bereavement Trust: www.bereavement-trust.org.uk — The Bereavement Trust recognises that evenings and nights can be especially difficult for the grief-stricken and therefore operates a 24/7, 365 days a year helpline open from 6:00pm to 10:00pm.

British Heart Foundation: www.bhf.org.uk — A leading British charity raising money to fund research into heart disease.

Carers Trust: www.carers.org — For those who find themselves caring for someone.

Carers UK: www.carersuk.org — As above.

Cruse: www.cruse.org.uk — Cruse is the UK's leading bereavement charity offering practical and emotional support to anybody grieving the loss of a loved one.

Kidney Care UK: www.kidneycare.org — Funding research into kidney disease.

Kidney Research UK: www.kidneyresearchuk.org — As above.

The Samaritans: www.samaritans.org — The Samaritans are open twenty-four hours a day every single day of the year to offer a compassionate, non-judgemental listening ear to those in any kind of emotional distress (not necessarily suicidal), including of course bereavement; there are local branches whose details can easily be found online but the (free) national helpline number is 116 123.

Widowed and Young: www.widowedandyoung.org.uk — WAY offers support to anybody under the age of fifty who has been widowed.

WAY Up: www.way-up.co.uk — The sister organisation to WAY for those widowed over the age of fifty.

More precious was the light in your eyes
than all the roses of the world.

—Edna St. Vincent Millay

'Twas my one Glory —
Let it be
Remembered
I was owned of Thee —

—Emily Dickinson

I am nothing special, of this I am sure. I am a common man with common thoughts and I've led a common life. There are no monuments dedicated to me and my name will soon be forgotten, but I've loved another with all my heart and soul, and to me, this has always been enough.

—Nicholas Sparks: *The Notebook*

All I can do, in what remains of my brief time,
is mention, to whoever cares to listen,
that a woman once existed, who was kind
and beautiful and brave, and I will not forget
how the world was altered, beyond recognition,
when we met.

—Michel Faber, 'Anniversary'

יזכור אלוהים

Printed and bound by CPI Group (UK) Ltd, Croydon, CR0 4YY